BATMAN™
RETURNS

BATMAN™
RETURNS

THE OFFICIAL MOVIE BOOK
MICHAEL SINGER

HAMLYN

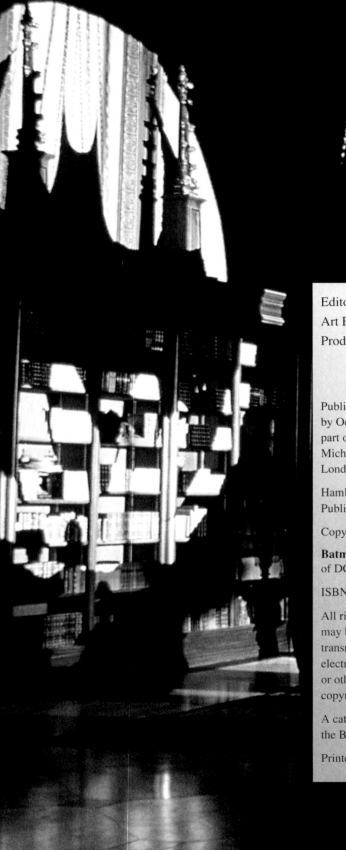

Editor Julian Brown
Art Editor Robin Whitecross
Production Controller Simon Shelmerdine

Published in 1992
by Octopus Illustrated Publishing
part of Reed International Books Limited
Michelin House, 81 Fulham Road,
London SW3 6RB

Hamlyn is an imprint of Octopus Illustrated
Publishing

A catalogue record for this book is available from
the British Library

Printed in Great Britain

CONTENTS

ACKNOWLEDGEMENTS

I'd like to express my gratitude to the 40 cast and crew members of *Batman Returns* who allowed me to thrust my tape recorder at them for interviews.

For their moral support, spiritual guidance and tangible assistance, endless thanks to Diane Minter, Jill Jacobs, Zade Rosenthal, Letitia Rogers, Alec Kamp, David McGiffert and his wonderful production staff, Ashley Fleming, Nansea Goldberg, Harry Colomby, Steve Shubin, Josh Levinson, Wendy Breck, Susan Robbins and the "Bat Babes", Karin McGaughey, everyone in Warner Bros.' Publicity Department and everyone at DC Comics Inc., Michael Klastorin, Mark Cotta Vaz, Jeff Walker, Marshall Silverman; and of course, good ol' Mom.

And, as my associates in a visionary Anglo-American *entente cordiale*, lavish cheerios to this book's editor, the ever-delightful Julian Brown, and the designer, the absolutely heavenly Robin Whitecross.

FOREWORD
by Tim Burton

It's often said that all beginnings are difficult, but they asked me to come up with one for this *Batman Returns* official movie book.

So let me begin by saying that *Batman Returns* is not really a sequel to *Batman*. It doesn't pick up where the first film left off. The sets for Gotham City are completely new. There are lots of new elements in the visuals and storyline that haven't been seen before. Even Batman's costume has been revised.

The point was to make it all feel fresh and new. It was the only way I could envision the movie.

One of the reasons I wanted to direct *Batman Returns* was to introduce different characters who are both very interesting and very complex, like The Penguin, Catwoman, Max Shreck and the Red Triangle Circus Gang. The *Batman* stories had some of the wildest characters in comics, yet for some reason, they seemed the most real to me. It's a challenge to make these characters come alive for movie audiences of the '90s.

If *Batman Returns* takes you to another place, another plane with its own reality, then I think we accomplished what we set out to do.

BATMAN RETURNS
Burton's Way

In a state called California, in a town called Burbank, in a studio called Warner Bros., in the courtyard of an unpretentious two-story, three-sided complex of offices, there is a volleyball court.

Not much of a court, really. Just a regulation-size net strung across a grassy knoll, the ground made somewhat hazardous by protruding pipes and precipitous potholes.

For several months in early-to-mid-1991, as the clock wound its way towards late afternoon/early evening and the Southern California sun began its crimson dip in the western sky, people started to emerge from their offices in the complex and took to this volleyball court like high school kids on a summer outing.

The requirements for participation were simple – if you wanted to play, you merely stepped onto the court. But once you were there, staunch teamwork, competitiveness and a spirit of fun were the order of the day. And when the light was lost, the players either retired to their desks for another hour (or three or four) of work, or called it a day and went home.

So what does all this have to do with Tim Burton and his new adventure epic, *Batman Returns*? If you will, call it Volleyball As A Metaphor For Creative Filmmaking.

Because the office complex was Producers Building 1, the production headquarters for *Batman Returns*, the players were various and sundry members of the crew, and arguably the most ferociously competitive player of the bunch was director Tim Burton – the man who brought Bob

Kane's legendary DC comic book character to screen life with *Batman*, one of the biggest hits in motion picture history.

These volleyball spectaculars proved to be representative of the overall mood of the entire *Batman Returns* shoot, of itself epic in nature: hard work, good fun, team spirit. And the director, as the commander of the production unit, set the tone for everything.

Burton's Background

Tim Burton is a unique phenomenon in the film world – a man with a singular and very personal vision who translates his wildly imaginative and wholly unexpected concepts to the screen without any compromise.

> **"In my mind, there are a lot of weird, interesting themes going on here. I've always been fascinated by what determines personality."**

Tim Burton consulting between takes with Michelle Pfeiffer and Michael Keaton (above) and the former cartoonist's personal vision of Batman, The Penguin and Catwoman (below).

Whether conjuring up a new direction for Danny DeVito (above), commanding from the Gotham City rooftops (opposite top), or collaborating with Michelle Pfeiffer (opposite bottom), Tim Burton was a man in constant cerebral and physical motion... a whirling dervish of creative energy.

Tim Burton is a man of stunning reputation. So far he has directed four feature films – *Pee-wee's Big Adventure* (1985), *Beetlejuice* (1985), *Batman* (1989) and *Edward Scissorhands* (1990) – each one of them very successful at the box office, all of them unique theatrical and visual entertainments. Originally trained in animation – a realm in which the creator's imagination has no limitations – Burton has continuously stretched the boundaries of live-action film.

Coincidentally, Burton was born and raised in Burbank, a typical suburban community which is also home to some show-business giants, such as Warner Bros., Universal, Disney, NBC-TV and several smaller production houses.

By his own definition a somewhat solitary youth, Burton became transfixed by old horror films (particularly *anything* starring his acknowledged hero, Vincent Price), and discovered his own formidable artistic talents. These were formally recognized in the ninth grade by local trash collectors when he won a prize for an anti-litter poster he designed (which adorned Burbank garbage trucks for a year thereafter).

Two dark-hued and dark-humored short

films, one animated – the delightful *Vincent*, about a lonely little boy's obsession with a horror movie star (any resemblance to reality was wholly intended) – and one live-action – *Frankenweenie*, a contemporary black-and-white riff on Mary Shelley's classic novel of regeneration – informed the once and future powers of Hollywood that an outlandish new talent was in their midst. They wasted little time in welcoming Burton to big-time Hollywood moviemaking.

From then to now, however, Tim Burton has not been tamed. The essence of kindliness on the set, Burton nevertheless has the energy and contained power of a wildcat, which he pours into filmmaking of the purest kind. Such matters as "image" are of little concern to Burton. Only "imagination" matters, and how it can be translated into visual and aural terms.

Burton Returns to Batman

After the massive success of his first Batman adventure, Tim Burton's many fans were delighted that he chose to expand the canvas of Gotham City and its inhabitants in *Batman Returns*. For Burton, however, directing the new film would give him a tremendous opportunity to fulfill his very particular vision of Batman, and the bizarre world and characters which surround him. In effect, the first *Batman* film was a first step, leading to this even more imaginative and entertaining adaptation of artist Bob Kane's eternally popular creation.

"Batman was one comic book where it just seemed that, as a whole, the characters were the most strange and interesting," notes Burton, while surveying construction on Bo Welch's massive Gotham Plaza set before the start of principal photography on *Batman Returns*. "Batman as a character seemed to have much more of a psychological foundation than any other comic book hero.

"Batman is a character who likes to

remain in the shadows," continues Burton. "He has a real split personality. You know, I always said that if he really knew who he was...if he had only gotten therapy...he probably wouldn't be doing what he does! So Batman is an odd character to portray because he's fairly remote and conflicted."

It was this understanding of Batman's complex essence which led Burton to cast Michael Keaton as the Dark Knight in the first *Batman*, realizing that a fully-dimensional portrayal was needed from a popular, accomplished, but decidedly offbeat movie star. At the time it was a highly controversial decision. Three years and more than 400-million worldwide box office dollars later, nobody any longer questions Burton's wisdom, or Keaton's abilities.

What excites the director about the new film is to further explore the Caped Crusader's heart and mind. "In the first movie, I felt that we arrived in the end at taking a new look at this character. So in *Batman Returns* – and I think Michael Keaton feels the same way – we're a little bit more comfortable in taking this foundation and then exploring it a little deeper.

"You know," Burton says with a mischievous smile, "doctors have spent years trying to analyze these characters. All three of the main figures in *Batman Returns* – Batman, Catwoman and The Penguin – are split right down the middle. There's a conflict between what they want to be versus what they *are*...what they look like versus what they *think* they look like...how they project themselves versus how they *really* come across.

"In my mind, there are a lot of weird, interesting themes going on here. I've always been fascinated by what determines personality. Is it in the genes? A child's upbringing? I mean, some kids seem just plain bad even before their parents get a chance to screw them up!"

Tim Burton took full advantage of his opportunities over the next several months, filming on some of the most intricate and astounding sets in American movie history, working with a veritable army of gifted performers, artists, stunt people, an enthusiastic crew and three great stars – Michael Keaton reprising his role as Batman & Bruce Wayne, Danny DeVito as The Penguin & Oswald Cobblepot and Michelle Pfeiffer as Catwoman & Selina Kyle. New standards in moviemaking were established on an almost daily basis, as an entire world unto itself was conjured up on seven soundstages at Warner Bros., another at nearby Universal and two large backlot exterior sets at Warner.

Casually dressed (usually in black, a favorite color shared by both Batman and Catwoman), alert to every detail as if tuning in to radio waves, Burton would carefully twist reality until it came into alignment with his own exceptional vision. The impossible became possible, the inconceivable conceivable, and the unbelievable, unbelievably believable!

It may all seem like a lot to handle for a man not yet out of his early 30s. But Tim Burton was the unqualified gentle master of a set that often resembled a three-ring circus, awash with all manner of people, animals, puppets, gadgets, special effects, buildings, and daily adventures in filmmaking for all concerned. After all, every circus needs a ringmaster.

WALKING THE TIGHTROPE
Denise Di Novi - Producer

In her relatively brief, but very successful career as a motion picture producer, Denise Di Novi has walked a swaying tightrope, unafraid to tempt the gods with films that are original, offbeat and often outrageous.

Partnered with Tim Burton for the past three years, Denise Di Novi produced *Edward Scissorhands* (1990), which proved artistically and financially fruitful.

Before Di Novi linked her fortunes with Burton, she first produced *Heathers* (1989) – the wittily subversive cult classic directed by Michael Lehmann and scripted by *Batman Returns* writer Daniel Waters – followed by the unquestionably strange and bizarre satire *Meet the Applegates* (1991), also directed by Lehmann, wherein a family of intergalactic cockroaches pose as an average all-American family.

Admitting to a preference for "character-driven, quirky" projects, it seems that all roads would inevitably lead Denise Di Novi to partnership with Burton. "Tim is unique in that he's a commercially successful director who doesn't make mainstream movies," says the young producer. "There's a simplicity and underlying sweetness to his work that embraces the outcast and differences in people. I think that's why his films are so accessible to moviegoers, and that certainly attracted me to working with him."

Despite her previous experiences as a producer – and having served in various production capacities on 15 other films – *Batman Returns* represents a quantum leap in responsibilities for Di Novi. "I don't think anybody dares to dream of producing a movie like this," she notes in her production trailer, just a few feet away from one of the Warner Bros. soundstages on which the film was becoming a reality.

"What was exciting to me about this movie was not only that it's such an extravaganza – which is a once-in-a-lifetime opportunity – but it's not merely big for big's sake. It's marrying artistic genius with scope, which is a rare thing."

There are few women in the history of Hollywood who have been charged with overseeing a project of such dimensions, but the eternally cool, calm and collected Di Novi never indicated any visible stress during the long and arduous shoot of *Batman Returns*.

"Making a movie is such a naturally chaotic process, and if the producer gets too excited, it only adds to that chaos. If you're in the middle of a hurricane and jump around too much, you'll get caught up in it. Instead, the producer has to be the eye of the hurricane, to balance rather than get swept away."

As if producing the biggest film of 1992 wasn't enough, Di Novi also had to continue overseeing the ongoing operations of Tim Burton Productions along with the company's hard-working production associates, Diane Minter and Jill Jacobs. All of them had to keep their fingers on the pulse of not only *Batman Returns*, but the organization's future projects as well.

This is all in a day's work for Denise Di Novi, who has grown accustomed to a titanic work load in search of movies that make a difference.

"I like films where within the first few frames, you can recognize that it's a David Cronenberg movie, or a Terry Gilliam movie – or a Tim Burton movie – just as you can instantly recognize a Claes Oldenburg or Roy Lichtenstein painting. Those are the works of art that are distinctive to me. And those are the kinds of films I like to make!"

THE BAT
THE CAT
THE PENGUIN

A Brief History

In the beginning, there was an 18-year-old kid cartoonist named Bob Kane.

A vintage photograph from 1943 shows Bob Kane (opposite top), barely out of his teens, doing what came naturally...creating and developing the legendary hero still going strong more than 50 years later! The selection of Batman comic book covers testifies to the Dark Knight's durability.

Laboring away in the jam-packed New York comic book and comic strip market of the late 1930s, the Bronx-born teenager began his professional career by drawing funny-fillers for the short-lived *Wow!* comic book, later contributing gag cartoons and a comedy-adventure strip about "Peter Pupp" for *Jumbo Comics*.

Kane then began making his first sales to the thriving DC Comics, mostly two-page comedy material like "Professor Doolittle," "Ginger Snap" and "Oscar the Gumshoe."

But one day, as if struck by lightning, Kane gazed upon a book about Leonardo Da Vinci which included drawings of many of the genius's futuristic inventions, including flying machines and parachutes.

"There was one drawing of a man on a kind of a sled with bat-wings called an Ornithopter," Kane recalls on the set of *Batman Returns*. "To me it made the man look like a bat. Funny...everybody else must have seen it, millions of people through the years, but I interpreted it into a new kind of comic book hero – a 'Bat-Man.'"

Thus, with the collaboration of writer and fellow teen Bill Finger, did Bob Kane create a new legend for the 20th century.

"From decade to decade Batman has been something special," wrote comic book historian Mark Cotta Vaz in his comprehensive *Tales of the Dark Knight*, chronicling the hero's first 50 years. "Stop a stranger on the street and just mention 'Batman' and they'll know who you're talking about."

The story of the creation of Batman has been oft-told, particularly since the 1989 release of Tim Burton's *Batman*, which fans saw as the first serious attempt to do the Dark Knight justice on film. Aficionados of the Caped Crusader were riveted by the adventure, visual majesty and psychological drama of the movie, which drained Batman of any hint of camp or cheap antics, without losing any of the shadowy humor which rings through the comic books or in DC's graphic novels, which appeared in the 1980s.

"When I created Batman at the very beginning I had no idea it would become such an event," notes Kane. "Batman just seems to hit a certain chord with people. It's not just fighting for justice against evil, it's the duality of Batman and the villains who confront them."

"The Bat-Man" (as he was originally called) first appeared in May 1939 – when *Detective Comics* introduced him in "The Case of the Chemical Syndicate." Kane and Finger proceeded to develop a magnificent array of bizarre, ingenious and frightening arch-villains. Some of them found their way onto the small screen in the 1960s (more on that later). One of his major characters, The Joker, was performed to malicious perfection by award-winning actor Jack Nicholson in the first *Batman* adventure.

In *Batman Returns*, two more of Kane's supremely original creations – The Penguin and Catwoman – are given unexpected new life, portrayed by two major movie stars born to play these roles, Danny DeVito and Michelle Pfeiffer.

Bob Kane, useful as ever, visits the Gotham Plaza set during production.

The Penguin

The Penguin, with his beak-like nose and incongruously elegant dress, first reared his distinctive head in late 1941. Bob Kane came up with the character from a less classical source than Leonardo Da Vinci.

"I haven't smoked in 40 years," claims the cartoonist, "but at the time I did, like everybody else in America. I thought smoking was cool, so I smoked Kool cigarettes. If you remember, the Kool cigarette pack had a drawing of a penguin on it. So when I was trying to invent some arch-villains for Batman to fight, I thought, 'Oh, my gosh! This penguin looks kind of like a little fat man in a tuxedo. Why not have a villain called The Penguin?'"

Like most of Kane's characters, The Penguin's persona and *modus operandi* have evolved quite a bit since his invention, but in the beginning he was clearly a cold-blooded killer (then again, in those early days, Batman himself thought little of dispatching his opponents to the hereafter). Later, The Penguin became more of a meticulous master crimesmith than a murderer, chastising his enemies (especially Batman) in overblown, high-faluting language and relying upon his astonishing array of trick umbrellas as weapons, tools, modes of transportation, even communication devices.

"When I created The Penguin in the comic book I thought he was comical-looking," remembers Kane. "And the idea that I made him a nefarious villain went against the typecast of what he looked like. I think that's part of his popularity, that this cartoonish character who looks so innocent is really a maniac. And therein lies the fascinating combination of good and evil."

Catwoman

Look under C in *The Encyclopedia of Comic Book Heroes* and you'll find Catwoman described as "daring and beautiful, whose costumes, special equipment, and choice of crimes all revolve around a feline theme."

Catwoman's history even pre-dates that of The Penguin, having made her comic book debut in mid-1940. Her real name is Selina Kyle (The Penguin's is the less musical Oswald Chesterfield Cobblepot). In *Batman Returns*, Selina is given a timely contemporary spin, as the much-oppressed assistant to Gotham mogul Max Shreck, suffering the slings and arrows of mean-spirited, sexist barbs launched at her from Max and his obnoxious son, Chip.

As with The Penguin and other arch-villains, Catwoman's personality has ebbed and flowed through the years, usually evil but sometimes not, with one consistency – her love/hate relationship with Batman, a theme very much explored in *Batman Returns*.

The physical origin of Catwoman was a combination of 1930s blonde bombshell Jean Harlow, the 1940s screen siren Hedy Lamarr, and Bob Kane's girlfriend at the time. "I admired Hedy Lamarr," recalls Kane, his eyes still twinkling these many years later. "She had that great feline beauty, and my girlfriend looked very much like her. My girlfriend was kind of handy as a seamstress, and she evolved a cat costume in which she posed as my model for the character."

Why a cat? "Well, a cat has nine lives," Kane emphasizes. "So I figured that whenever she was caught, or wounded, she would survive and live again for another go-round with Batman. Also, I feel there's something very mysterious about cats, and I equate that with women."

The Penguin and Catwoman on Film

Curiously enough, neither The Penguin nor Catwoman were featured characters in the first filmizations of Batman, Columbia Pictures' low-budget black-and-white serials in 1943 and 1949.

The live-action, stupendously campy television series that aired on ABC-TV from January 1966 to March 1968, however, gave both The Penguin and Catwoman extensive screen time. Burgess Meredith, a fine and serious actor, was a popular Penguin of his day, generally acknowledged as everybody's favorite villain in that particular manifestation of Batman.

It took not one, but three successive actresses to fill Catwoman's claws: first the athletic Julie Newmar, followed by the sultry Lee Meriwether, and then by the aptly-named singer Eartha Kitt. Meredith and Meriwether would portray their respective characters in 20th Century-Fox's splashy 1966 film version of the television series.

It would take a fine detective, though, to draw a direct line from those pop art-era evocations of The Penguin and Catwoman to their brand-new interpretations by Danny DeVito and Michelle Pfeiffer. Just as Tim Burton and his actors in the first *Batman* restored power, terror and psychological validity to the Dark Knight and The Joker, so do the director and his players take Batman, The Penguin and Catwoman into the '90s with *Batman Returns*.

To begin with, Burton and screenwriter Daniel Waters developed new origins for both characters, haunting and humorous, tinged with tragedy and contemporary sensibilities.

Although The Penguin and Catwoman remain essentially true to their essence – Bob Kane's ex-girlfriend would be proud to know that in the new film, Catwoman's costume is also home-sewn; and the Penguin still has that fabulous arsenal of evil umbrellas – they are now spirited in utterly new directions.

And that's fine with Bob Kane, the father of them all. "When I created Batman and the related characters, he was a dark, brooding vigilante. It all became campy and comedic in the '60s with the advent of the TV show.

"But if I had my wishes, I'd rather have the mysterioso, profound Batman characters. The first *Batman* movie brought them back to whence they came. Tim Burton is a wonderful director," concludes Kane, "and he brings great visual atmosphere to his movies. He and I think alike, and Batman was depicted exactly the way I created him in the beginning. It's dark, it's textured, but it's also a lot of fun...and I like that."

So did millions of moviegoers around the world, added to the millions who have relished Bob Kane's brilliant comic book creations for more than half a century.

The past and the present: Bob Kane's sketches of Batman (above) drawn previous to the character's first DC Comics appearance in 1939; and panels from the 1991 graphic novel (below) "Catwoman: Her Sister's Keeper."

BATMAN
Michael Keaton

"Instead of falling back on superhero cliches, I had a vision of who Batman could be on film. It was a good case of trusting my beliefs and instincts."

Bruce Wayne, a man with a deeply divided soul, keeps an electronic eye on Gotham City in the Batcave (above); and in his alter-ego of the Dark Knight, he confronts his nemesis and kindred spirit, Catwoman (below)

Take a good, close look at Michael Keaton. Now look again, and chances are that you won't see the same person twice.

Take a look at Keaton as Billy Blaze, the morgue attendant he portrayed in *Night Shift* (1982), his first major big screen appearance; the middle-class Mr. Nice Guy in *Mr. Mom* (1983); a self-absorbed hockey player in *Touch and Go* (1986); the small town guy trying to save their auto factory in *Gung Ho* (1986); a supernatural "bio-exorcist" in Tim Burton's wildly successful *Beetlejuice* (1988); substance abuser Daryl Poynter in the starkly dramatic *Clean and Sober* (1988); a mental patient in *The Dream Team* (1989); the chillingly psychopathic tenant in *Pacific Heights* (1990); or, for that matter, the powerful Dark Knight in *Batman*. Can all of these characters *really* be played by the same guy?

That is what marks Michael Keaton as unique in his generation of American male movie stars. Forget about definitions like "comic actor," "dramatic actor," "adventure actor." Keaton is a consummate actor, blessed with the full capability of playing any conceivable character. With him, anything is not only possible, but probable.

When you take this extraordinary versatility, and combine it with Keaton's natural charisma, you get a major screen personality who is defined not by his "type," but rather by his stubborn refusal to be "typed" at all.

In the light of the film's massive worldwide success, it may seem hard to believe that by accepting Tim Burton's offer to portray *Batman* in the first film, Keaton was taking a tough leap over an extremely risky hurdle. Although Keaton had already displayed an utter unpredictability in his career choice, audiences didn't automatically think of him as the superhero type.

Of course, that was exactly why Burton wanted Keaton for *Batman*. The idea was to create a character that was recognizable as a human being rather than a fashion model. (As it turned out, however, all agreed that Keaton looked great as both Batman *and* Bruce Wayne).

Was Keaton aware of the risks he was taking? Of course he was. "I looked at the script of *Batman*, considered who was involved, and my instincts told me that it was huge. Now, huge means a lot to an actor. If *Batman* succeeded, it could be a huge success. But if it failed, it could be a huge failure. Not only it – but *me*!

"Maybe I never really stopped to consider what could have happened to my career if it had bombed...but I usually trust my instincts, and my instincts told me that I knew how to play this character, and I trusted Tim's vision."

Above: Batman and The Penguin finally face off in front of Shreck's Department Store in Gotham Plaza. Opposite: Using his extended glider wings, Batman soars from high above the city in a sequence shot on the tremendous "Downtown Gotham City" backlot set.

Burton knew...Keaton knew...but the public still wondered if the actor could pull it off. And it wasn't until midway through the shoot of the first *Batman* that Keaton came to realize that there were waves of doubt wafting over the Atlantic to the soundstages of Pinewood Studios in England.

"There was something in that negative response that stirred in me what I'm going to call a healthy 'attitude,' which is different from an unhealthy 'attitude,'" says Keaton with an ironic smile. "I secretly liked the challenge, and was determined to prove that I could nail it."

Time has told, and history has judged. Audiences and critics alike agreed that Keaton found the perfect combination of qualities that allowed *Batman* to spring from the pages of the DC Comics magazines into a multi-dimensional, utterly believable, big screen character. Brooding, magnetic,

enigmatic, lonely, humorous, appealing – this was a Batman with emotional depth and a real edge.

Despite the fact that the veteran crew of *Batman Returns* had all seen the first movie, nearly everyone took one step backward when Michael Keaton arrived on the set for the first time in his Batman costume. Once in the outfit, Keaton's stature seemed to grow by several inches. It's all in the body language.

"When you're in the suit," remarks Keaton, "you feel and act differently. Also, you're very isolated in the Batman suit, which is great. On the first *Batman*, I really used that isolation to help create the character, who feels cut off from the mainstream."

Batman is less verbal and more physical. Bruce Wayne is less physical and more verbal. In both cases, Keaton had an opportunity to work with the full range of his acting

skills. "Ironically, I've only done a few films – like *Beetlejuice*, *Batman* and maybe *One Good Cop* (1991) – which really allowed me to be physical," explains Keaton. "But I was a very physical kid, I still love sports, and my first heroes were the guys on TV who were involved in a lot of action."

For *Batman* and *Batman Returns*, Keaton underwent a rigorous training program with British-born martial arts/kickboxing champion Dave Lea, learning the swift, lethal moves which make Batman such a fighting machine. "Michael was an incredibly fast learner on the first *Batman*," says Lea, "and by now there isn't much more I can teach him."

Out of the Batman costume and into his Bruce Wayne togs, Keaton was able to relax a little more on the set, amiably chatting with the cast and crew between takes. But the actor found that after a three-year interval, returning to the character was not quite as simple

as one may think. "It's *Batman*, but it's also a completely different movie," remarks Keaton. "I had to be careful that I wasn't doing an imitation of Michael Keaton playing Batman and Bruce Wayne...I had to *become* those characters once again, without anything else getting in the way.

"Why am I playing Batman a second time? Well, I've never played the same character twice, which is a challenge, and it's real interesting to take it further along. Also, Tim takes everyone on a fantastic voyage...and I'm totally with him on this quest."

Michael Keaton – an actor who defies definition but who managed to re-define Batman for a generation – is also on his own quest: to constantly experiment, expand his range as an actor, ignore safe choices and confound conventional expectations.

After all, as Keaton admits, "I usually am a person who goes his own route."

THE PENGUIN
Danny DeVito

> "The Penguin, had he been understood and nurtured, could have been another Einstein. Unfortunately, he's a product of his physical appearance."

Above: The Penguin fires another salvo of bullets from his umbrella-gun at the Maxsquerade Ball. Right: The Penguin wields the "Pied Piper" umbrella in his eerie Lair.

It seems that everyone who worked on *Batman Returns* has a favorite Danny DeVito story, but this is the one that's recalled more often than any other. It was *very* early in the morning on the Gotham Plaza set (not much after midnight), toward the tail end of a long working day. Spirits were flagging, bodies were drooping, when suddenly – it was The Penguin to the rescue!

Standing beneath the strange and soaring towers of Gotham Cathedral, Danny DeVito – attired in full Penguin make-up and costume – launched into a non-stop half-hour of impromptu stand-up comedy during a break, regaling cast and crew with one snappy, ribald joke after another. The laughter had a more tonic effect on those assembled than five cups of high-octane espresso. Resuscitated by DeVito's nimble wit, everyone caught their second (or third) wind and ploughed through the rest of the night's work until "Wrap!" was finally called.

That night, Danny DeVito was utilizing his humor and humanity to keep things moving, as the consummate professional that he is. For with his portrayal of The Penguin in *Batman Returns*, DeVito adds yet another vivid characterization to his already extraordinary gallery of performances. DeVito has emerged not only as one of America's most

versatile leading men, but also a noted film-maker, as the director of *Throw Momma From the Train* (1987) and *The War of the Roses* (1989). Immediately upon completion of his work in *Batman Returns*, DeVito rushed into pre-production on his biggest directing assignment yet – *Hoffa*, the story of the controversial labor leader which stars Jack Nicholson.

Stardom hasn't come easily for DeVito. He put enormous time and effort into theatre and small film roles before winning national recognition in the Oscar-winning *One Flew Over the Cuckoo's Nest* (1975), then solidifying his popularity with an Emmy and Golden Globe-winning performance as Louie De Palma in "Taxi," one of the most famous characters in American television history.

Since then, in addition to appearances in his own directorial achievements, DeVito has starred in such smash hits as *Romancing the Stone* (1984), *The Jewel of the Nile* (1985), *Ruthless People* (1986), *Tin Men* (1987) and *Twins* (1988). Most recently, he starred as the corporate raider Lawrence "Larry the Liquidator" Garfield in *Other People's Money* (1991), and next played the title role of *Jack the Bear* (1992).

For *Batman Returns*, DeVito faced the exciting challenge of discovering the penguin inside the man, and the man inside the penguin. As conceived by Tim Burton, the screenwriters and Danny DeVito, The

Penguin is neither human nor fowl, but rather a terrifying combination of both.

DeVito discussed the role on his next-to-last day of filming, as his Penguin make-up and hair applications – which took more than two hours to apply each morning – were carefully removed by Oscar-winning make-up artist Ve Neill and hair stylist Yolanda Toussieng. "It's being peeled off as we speak," said DeVito, "and it's such a strange feeling. Right now, after wearing it for some 60 days, for 12 to 15 hours a day, I've been looking at myself more as The Penguin than as Danny. When the make-up's put on, it's so organic that it just becomes part of you."

Indeed, DeVito was so engrossed in the total being of The Penguin during filmmaking, that he almost never broke character while in make-up and costume. Even on-set conversations with Tim Burton were held in The Penguin's utterly distinctive voice, very different from DeVito's familiar articulations.

In *Batman Returns*, The Penguin – and his more "respectable" identity of Oswald Cobblepot – gain considerable dimension from what has been seen before. DeVito has excelled in finding intrinsic humanity in characters which he perceives as having been misunderstood by others.

Remarks Tim Burton about Danny DeVito: "I don't think there's anybody better at making the horrible acceptable. I feel like a real kindred spirit with Danny, and I think we're really creating something that people will see and enjoy as a natural expansion of the comic book character."

"The Penguin is a very intelligent man," declares DeVito, "someone who always wanted acceptance. He's a guy who is living one world in his mind and another as people perceive him. I mean, his parents took a look at him when he was a baby and totally rejected him. But if they tried to understand that there was a human being inside that hideous 'penguin boy,' he might have become another Albert Einstein.

"He could have been nurtured, gone to the best schools and become a worldly human being," continued the actor. "But from the confines of the Lair in which he was raised and the underworld of characters to which he was exposed, The Penguin became what he is."

On the set, DeVito was fearlessly physical. When the citizens of Gotham pelt The Penguin with a colorful and odious assortment of fruits, vegetables and eggs, the actor refused a stand-in. Instead, he took the full brunt of the veg-attack himself, splattered with the gooey results in take after take. When The Penguin hurriedly speeds his Rubber Duck Vehicle up the steep steps of his subterranean lair, DeVito again insisted on living dangerously rather than relying on a stuntman.

And when the time came for The Penguin to hang up his umbrellas and DeVito to bid the crew farewell ("It's a sad day in Gotham," quipped one of the production assistants, echoing a widely-held sentiment), the actor gave a rousing goodbye speech – as The Penguin, of course.

After all, as Danny DeVito pronounced in the make-up trailer with a smile and a flourish, "All the world's a stage, and The Penguin's on it!"

Main: With Max Shreck imprisoned in a giant bird cage, The Penguin addresses his aquatic troops.
Above left: In his guise of the respectable Oswald Cobblepot, The Penguin pores over papers in Gotham City's Hall of Records.

CATWOMAN
Michelle Pfeiffer

"For me, Catwoman just broke all the stereotypes of what it meant to be a woman. She certainly was a childhood heroine of mine."

Call it what you will – fate, karma, destiny, fortune, providence, kismet – there was no way that Michelle Pfeiffer would go through life and *not* play Catwoman!

"Catwoman certainly was a childhood heroine of mine," the actress admits with a distinctively feline glow. "I used to watch the TV series and just wait for her to come on, and she was never on enough as far as I was concerned."

And lest one think that the talented and tremendously respected multiple-award-winning Pfeiffer just waits for any and all offers to roll in, she adds that "when the first *Batman* went into production, I called a couple of people I knew who were working on the movie and told them to tell Tim Burton that I wanted to play Catwoman. I said please, I'll do it for free! One scene, a cameo...anything!"

Well, in between the first *Batman* and *Batman Returns*, Tim Burton must have come into cosmic alignment with Pfeiffer's thinking. Catwoman is one of the movie's trinity of major characters, along with the Dark Knight and The Penguin. Michelle Pfeiffer, in the role which she coveted for so many years, emerges as Catwoman's ultimate incarnation. As conceived and written, Catwoman is a deeply complex character, incorporating in one disjointed soul the oppressed and the avenger, the desperately needy and the ferociously independent, the kitten and the lioness!

What did Michelle Pfeiffer find so appealing and fascinating about Catwoman when she was first introduced to the character? "I guess she just broke all of the stereotypes of what it meant to be a woman," she recalls. "I found that shocking and titillating and forbidden. Also, I was probably at the age where I was really coming into my own sexuality, and I just found Catwoman thrilling to watch."

Michelle Pfeiffer was also thrilling to watch as she created the twin roles of Catwoman and Selina Kyle, throwing herself into the maelstrom of an extremely demanding part. Pfeiffer not only had to tack down the dramatically different traits of Catwoman and Selina in a pure acting sense, she also had to become an expert in both martial arts and the whip to carry out the extraordinarily difficult action sequences, training for several hours a day months before filming started.

Notes Anthony De Longis, Pfeiffer's whip trainer, "Michelle is using the whip exactly as Catwoman would. It's sensual, sinuous, sexual and dangerous. Michelle and the whip really complement each other. Her movements are unique and special, and she's doing things with the bullwhip that Indiana Jones never dreamed of!"

Adds kickboxing champion Kathy Long, who trained Pfeiffer in martial arts: "Michelle is an absolute perfectionist. If she doesn't get it right the first time, she'll keep

Above: In one of their quieter moments together, Selina Kyle and Bruce Wayne share a dance at the Maxsquerade Ball. Below: With whip and chair in hand, Catwoman could tame a lion...or attempt to tame Batman. Opposite inset: The Penguin and Catwoman formulate a scheme to defeat Batman and conquer Gotham City. Opposite: By day, a haunted Selina Kyle wanders through Gotham Plaza.

on and on until she aces it. She's a woman with incredible determination."

Pfeiffer in her sleek, shiny, seductive and threatening Catwoman costume was a sight to behold, and everyone was amazed at how easily Pfeiffer found it to walk on those nasty-looking five-inch-tall spike heels, let alone punching, kicking and twirling in them!

Then again, Michelle Pfeiffer has always been full of surprises. Blessed with a transcendent beauty that often *limits* an actress's potential, Pfeiffer has in fact fought a hard, uphill struggle towards her well-earned place in the ranks of America's most popular, accomplished and honored actresses.

After starring in such early-career films as *Grease 2* (1982), *Scarface* (1983), *Into the Night* (1985), *Ladyhawke* (1985) and *Sweet Liberty* (1986), Pfeiffer began to expand her range and reputation in *The Witches of Eastwick* (1987), *Married to the Mob* (1988) and *Tequila Sunrise* (1988). Then Pfeiffer was cast by director Stephen Frears to portray Madame de Tourvel in *Dangerous Liaisons* (1988). The role not only firmly established Pfeiffer's luminous artistry and versatility, but also brought her an Academy Award nomination.

The following year, Pfeiffer knocked out audiences and critics around the world with her performance as slinky nightclub singer Susie Diamond in *The Fabulous Baker Boys* (1989), which showcased Pfeiffer's singing as well as acting talent. It also resulted in her winning the New York Film Critics, Los Angeles Film Critics and National Society of

Film Critics awards as Best Actress, as well as a second Academy Award nomination.

Most recently, Pfeiffer starred in Fred Schepisi's *The Russia House* (1990) and *Love Field* (1992). As the tough-talking coffee shop waitress in *Frankie and Johnny*, she received a 1991 Golden Globe nomination.

And yet, with all that's come before, Pfeiffer notes: "It's ironic that Catwoman might be the most difficult role I've ever played. We're trying to do something more than a two-dimensional comic-book character, and I approach it as seriously as I would any role.

"The character of Catwoman and Selina Kyle deals with duality, and I think that people in general – and women in particular – have a hard time accepting both their light and dark sides. I just find Catwoman to be an amazingly powerful, moving, funny and very touching character. I've loved playing her."

And one final question. Is Michelle Pfeiffer more attracted to Catwoman or Selina Kyle? "When I'm doing Catwoman and flying with that, I'm really loving Catwoman," she responds. "And when I'm kind of goofy and falling apart as Selina, I'm having a really great time with her.

"But," adds Pfeiffer decisively, "I know that when I play Scrabble by myself, Catwoman *always* wins!"

MAX SHRECK Christopher Walken

It may be possible that in the universal scheme of things, there is a role that Christopher Walken is incapable of playing.

On second thought...maybe not. During the course of his wildly versatile career, Walken has demonstrated an aptitude for a mind-boggling range of performances, from his early career as a dancer to his much-honored stage performances, on to his work in television and motion pictures. In fact, Walken's portrayal of a tormented Vietnam soldier in Michael Cimino's *The Deer Hunter* (1978) brought him an Academy Award for Best Supporting Actor.

While it's true that Walken has portrayed villains before – in the films *A View to a Kill* (1985), *At Close Range* (1986) and, arguably, in *King of New York* (1991) – no two performances have been the same, or even resemble each other. Noted for his utter spontaneity on the set, Walken is loathe to repeat himself.

The secret to playing scoundrels, according to the actor, is the fact that bad guys never really think they're bad. "I think they believe that they're doing some sort of service in the big picture," says Walken between camera set-ups in the spectacular Shreck Industries office set, fully attired in striped three-piece suit, black gloves, elegant spats and gray wig.

Max Shreck is Gotham City's prime mover and shaker, the real power behind the throne, and a flamboyant satire of the all-American robber barons who cut a haughty swath through all branches of society, marrying industry, politics and power to achieve frightful ends. Rather than play up the more hysterical aspects of Shreck's character however, Walken characteristically chose a more subtle path. "You have to look for human

qualities, even in people who have inhuman characteristics," Walken explains. "I think that Max probably didn't have a lot of formal education. He sort of made his own way, and really believes it when he says 'There's no such thing as too much power.'"

Walken even admits to sharing one of Shreck's most apparent traits: "He has a kind of single-mindedness that I suppose I have too. He's very tenacious, and so am I."

Filmgoers who have appreciated Walken's performances not only in the above-mentioned films, but also *Annie Hall* (1977), *The Dead Zone* (1983), *Biloxi Blues* (1988), *The Milagro Beanfield War* (1988) and such TV movies as *Who Am I This Time?* (1982) and *Sarah, Plain and Tall* (1991), would have to admit that single-mindedness can get you somewhere.

And yes, to those observant film buffs who know and love silent movies, the name

> **"Is Max a bad guy? I guess you have to say that. But bad guys probably think they're doing some sort of service in the big picture."**

"Max Shreck" is indeed an intentional homage to Max Schreck, the German actor who played the title role in F.W. Murnau's classic 1922 vampire film *Nosferatu*. In that movie, Max Schreck sucked blood. In *Batman Returns*, Max Shreck sucks up money. Schreck and Shreck are distant cousins, one letter removed!

ALFRED
Michael Gough

Here's one for the *Batman Returns* "What A Coincidence!" file: Michael Gough, the gloriously elegant British actor who returns to his role as Bruce Wayne's impeccable butler and unflappable friend, admits that he founded the character of Alfred on a real person.

"Yes, I based Alfred on someone that I know in England. When he was in the British Army, years ago, this man was a military butler to a major general. After the officer lost a leg in wartime and left the service, this butler continued looking after him and his family at home. Then, when the major general died, the butler remained to look after his widow. He is totally upright, totally devoted and a very loyal servant...just like Alfred."

That's right – Michael Gough based Alfred on a "batman," which is British parlance for a military butler.

Throughout his venerable 53-year career, Gough has graced hundreds of films, plays and TV programs with his extraordinary flexibility as a performer. Whatever the task, Gough has always been right on target. His myriad portrayals have been seen in such English screen classics over the years as *Anna Karenina* (1948), *The Man in the White Suit* (1951), Laurence Olivier's *Richard III* (1955), *The Horse's Mouth* (1958), *Women in Love* (1969) and *The Go-Between* (1971). Gough's more recent films have included *The Dresser* (1983), *Top Secret!* (1984) and *Out of Africa* (1985).

But to a generation of fans – including an admiring young Tim Burton – Gough is perhaps best known as the star of a series of horror films for Hammer and other British studios which brought him permanent cult-actor status to aficionados of that genre. Who can forget Gough in such blood-chilling epics as *Horror of Dracula* (1958), *Konga* (1961), *The Black Zoo* (1962), *The Phantom of the Opera* (1962), *The Skull* (1965), *Berserk* (1967) and *Trog* (1970)!

Gough plays a quite different personage in the two *Batman* films, however. Alfred, according to the actor, is "an old fashioned man who tries to bring up Bruce Wayne like a little gentleman. Because, as a boy, Bruce

> **"Alfred would have done anything to make sure Bruce Wayne was going to be looked after and lead a good life – just as a real father would."**

> **"If it wasn't for Batman, Gordon would need two more batallions of policemen."**

lost both of his parents, Alfred has the great responsibility of being both substitute father *and* mother to the boy."

Because Alfred is the only one who really knows Bruce Wayne, he's not only a trusted friend, but also an active co-combatant in Batman's fight against crime in Gotham City. *Batman Returns* gives Alfred – and Michael Gough – more of an opportunity to display the butler's ingenuity and courage.

COMMISSIONER GORDON
Pat Hingle

Below: Two of Gordon's men take shots at Batman, wrongly believing that the Caped Crusader has taken a detour into villainy.
Right: The Mayor comforts his wife after The Penguin – in collusion with Max Shreck – "rescues" their baby.

Commissioner Gordon has become more dependent on help from Batman," explains Pat Hingle of the character he created in the first film. "If it weren't for Batman, Gordon would need about two more batallions of policemen to control the city."

Hingle, one of the top handful of great American character actors, superbly embodied Gordon's gruffness and compassion in *Batman*. As many actors do with their, Hingle created a personal "backstory" to explain Gordon's bond of understanding with the Caped Crusader.

"The way I see it," Hingle declares, "Gordon was just a cop on the beat when the young Bruce Wayne watched his parents gunned down. Gordon was the first one to get to the scene of the crime. Somehow, when Batman made his first appearances in Gotham City, Gordon knew that he had seen this person before."

Although Gordon was reluctant to believe stories of the mysterious sightings of a man dressed as a bat in the first film, by now "Gordon makes no effort to downplay Batman's contribution. The Commissioner regards Batman as a colleague."

Hingle recently passed his 40th year in show business, a career which has seen him star in countless plays, movies and television programs. Four of his 22 Broadway shows were Pulitzer Prize winners; his screen credits include such fine films as *On the Waterfront* (1954), *Splendor in the Grass* (1961), *Norma Rae* (1979), *The Falcon and the Snowman* (1985) and *The Grifters* (1990).

And here's another one for the "What A Coincidence!" file: in 1974, Hingle co-starred in a movie called *Super Cops*, about two New York City policemen whose unorthodox methods of battling crime earn them the familiar names: Batman and Robin!

To portray the Mayor of Gotham City – a man faced with the impossible task of keeping law and order in a city which frequently knows neither – Tim Burton chose an actor of vast talents and wide experience: Michael Murphy.

Murphy is no stranger to playing political figures. In fact, he starred in the title role of *Tanner '88*, a highly praised Home Box Office series which ran during the 1988 U.S. presidential election. The you-are-there style satire, directed by Robert Altman and written by cartoonist Garry "Doonesbury" Trudeau, had a lot of Americans believing that Jack Tanner was just as real as his fellow candidates.

"The Mayor is different from Tanner," says Murphy. "Running Gotham City is even tougher than running America. He's basically a decent guy, but there's so much crime, civil disobedience and deceit in Gotham City that the Mayor is inevitably in over his head."

One of the few things the Mayor can fall back on is Gotham City's nocturnal avenger. "He's put a lot of his eggs in Batman's basket," notes Murphy of the Mayor, "and he relies on him to bail the city out."

Murphy has become famous as a jack-of-all-trades whose talents have been enlisted

THE MAYOR Michael Murphy

by some of the world's more celebrated filmmakers. He was a member of Robert Altman's unofficial repertory company, having appeared in four of that director's features, including *M*A*S*H* (1970) and *Nashville* (1975).

Several of Murphy's films have cast the actor in roles of morally dubious characters, including the unfaithful husband in *An Unmarried Woman* (1978), the sleazy journalist in *The Year of Living Dangerously* (1982) and perhaps most famously as Woody Allen's philandering best friend in *Manhattan* (1979).

"Yes, I was the original whining Yuppie," jokes the actor.

But, in fact, Michael Murphy is one of the least-complaining and hardest-working of American actors.

"The Mayor's a decent man, but there's so much going on beyond his control that it makes it impossible for him to properly run Gotham City."

THE ICE PRINCESS
Cristi Conaway

"She's a celebrity in her own mind. As long as you don't mess up her make-up, you can talk to her."

S he's a celebrity in her own mind," says the classically blonde and beauteously proportioned Cristi Conaway of the Ice Princess, the character she so ably embodies in *Batman Returns*.

Rarely has such a sweet, talented and co-operative person been called upon to essay a role of one so utterly opposite. "I don't think she's as nasty as her title may sound," adds Conaway with an understanding smile. "As long as you don't mess up her make-up, you can talk to her."

Considering what happens to the Ice Princess in *Batman Returns*, you'd feel a lot sorrier for her if she wasn't the type to shove little old ladies to the pavement to save her own (admittedly beautiful) skin. The embodiment of mindless glamor, the Ice Princess is a total contrast to Cristi Conaway, whose intelligence presents a fine match for her radiant good looks.

Since arriving in Hollywood two years ago from her native Texas, Conaway has been steadily building her career with roles of increasing importance. Following completion of her physically demanding work in *Batman Returns* – the unfortunate Ice Princess undergoes everything from kidnapping by The Penguin to getting kicked off a chair by Catwoman – Conaway immediately segued to a major part in Woody Allen's latest movie.

But try as she might, Conaway just couldn't find any real profundity hidden just beneath the Ice Princess's surface. "I don't think she's particularly well-read," declares the actress of her fictitious character. "But I think she's read every issue of *Vogue* that was ever published!"

CHIP SHRECK
Andrew Bryniarski

I f the first task of a good actor is to know his character, then Andrew Bryniarski has Chip Shreck pegged to a tee: "He's a creep. He's a jerk. He's a sexist. He's a young guy with money, power, a future, but not a lot of time for anyone else but his father."

It might also be mentioned that Chip is 6 feet 4 inches tall, weighs about 250 lb (all muscle) and totally dedicated to his dad – Gotham's monumental mogul Max Shreck, played by Christopher Walken.

In his very new and highly promising

career, Bryniarski has thus far specialized in playing very big guys with a comic edge. Before winning the role of Chip in *Batman Returns*, Bryniarski tossed the pigskin in the football comedy *Necessary Roughness* (1991) and portrayed the aptly named Agent Butterfinger in *Hudson Hawk* (1991).

Quite the opposite of his yuppie-from-hell *Batman Returns* character, the endlessly good-humored and affable Byrniarski developed a passion for body-building in his formative years. Gifted in football, martial arts, horse jumping and marksmanship, his determined efforts eventually landed him the title of "Teenage Mr. USA" in 1988.

Bryniarski's successful transition to acting was made carefully and with a good deal of determination. "I won't do anything until I've educated myself and have enough confidence," states the young actor. "But once I decide to put my name on it, I've got to be in it to win. No retreat, no surrender."

THE RED TRIANGLE
Circus Gang

Every child knows something his parents forget – that circuses can be downright *scary*, with clowns the scariest of all! This is something that Tim Burton must have understood from his childhood, since terrifying clowns appear in most of his films, including *Pee-wee's Big Adventure* (Pee-wee's nightmares about his bicycle), *Beetlejuice* (during the phantasmagoric climax) and even *Batman* (The Joker's mime-thugs).

For those of you who share Burton's ambivalence toward these peculiar entertainments, hold on to your popcorn – the Red Triangle Circus Gang has come to Gotham! What a circus, and what a gang: garish carnival colors adorning everything from their tattered raiment and second-hand vehicles to a deceptively innocent-looking arsenal.

The story of *Batman Returns* reveals that in times past, the Red Triangle Circus Gang amused Gotham and its delighted children, until reports of missing youngsters forced the troupe to fold its tents. And before he could be questioned, at least one performer vanished, to emerge years later as their un-qualified general of mayhem: The Penguin.

If The Penguin is the general, then the Organ Grinder – portrayed by one of America's most accomplished character actors, Vincent Schiavelli, whose credits include *Ghost* (1990), *Amadeus* (1984) and *One Flew Over the Cuckoo's Nest* (1975) – is the major. "The members of the Circus Gang are all societal outcasts," maintains Schiavelli, "and they recognize a kindred spirit in The Penguin. He was someone they could look up to, because of his intellect and special relationship to animals."

The Organ Grinder, of course, has a monkey for a companion (don't all organ

> **"The Red Triangle Circus Gang is like a group of religious fanatics. And The Penguin is their religion."**

> **"Chip is a creep, a jerk and a sexist. But at least he loves his father."**

grinders?), eager to do his master's bidding. He also has a gatling gun in his organ, which most organ grinder's *don't* have. Another core member of the gang, the Poodle Lady – portrayed by the elegant and haunting Swiss-born actress Anna Katarina, herself a former circus performer in Europe – has a ratty poodle (what else?).

The other chief Red Triangle Circus Gang thugs include the Tattooed Strongman (Rick Zumwalt); Knife-thrower Dame (Erika Andersch); Fat Clown (Travis McKenna); Thin Clown (Doug Jones); Snake Woman (played by a real snake woman, succinctly named Flame); and as the Sword-Swallower, John Strong, a man who grew up under the tents of his father's Big John Strong Circus, and who holds the *Guinness Book of Record*s title for the most number of swords swallowed at one time – eleven!

They're aided and abetted by an array of auxiliary circus thugs portrayed by a talented group of stuntplayers and real-life circus people, all helping to fulfill our worst childhood nightmares of what really lurks beneath the big top.

Top left: The agile Acrobat Thug holds the "kidnapped" Mayor's baby.
Bottom left: The rail-like Thin Clown installs a tracking device into the Batmobile's mighty engine.
Main: The Red Triangle Circus Gang's core members – The Organ Grinder (with pipe), Tattooed Strongman, Poodle Lady, Thin Clown, Fat Clown and Snake Woman. This is not a sideshow you'd want to visit your town!

'T is the week before Christmas, and for once the citizens of Gotham City try to put aside their daily woes of living in one of the world's most crime-ridden cities to enjoy the holiday season. On a podium overlooking the massive Gotham Plaza, the Mayor of the City (Michael Murphy) is presenting "Gotham's own Santa Claus" Max Shreck (Christopher Walken). In fact, Shreck is more Scrooge than Santa, but with son Chip (Andrew Bryniarski) by his side, he delivers an unctuously self-effacing speech before tossing little wrapped Christmas presents to the crowd. Suddenly, Max, Chip and the Mayor notice an enormous Christmas present being wheeled into the Plaza. "Great idea," says the Mayor admiringly. "But not mine," responds a mystified Max. And from a shadowy figure half-seen through a sewer grate, as if a signal, comes the threatening croak, "Deck the halls."

Suddenly, the giant Christmas present explodes in a cataclysm of confetti, and like the Trojan Horse of old, releases its contents – the colorfully attired and absolutely malicious Red Triangle Circus Gang, including the evil Organ Grinder (Vincent Schiavelli) and his equally odious compatriots.

At the moment of the explosion, five acrobat thugs are projected through the skies of Gotham with the greatest of ease, hurling more than 100 feet to their intended targets: one strikes a policeman on horseback; another plunges into the Plaza's 35-foot tall Christmas tree; the third smacks right into a department store Santa Claus; another knocks over a group of Victorian-dressed Christmas carollers; and the fifth lands on a leg of one of the two gigantic statues at either end of the tunnel leading into the Plaza. Mayhem ensues as other members of the Circus Gang – including three death's-head-helmeted motorcyclists, flame-juggling stilt-walkers and a Satanic firebreather – wreak havoc among Gotham's citizenry.

Finally, a toy sled smashes into a police car window...inside Police Commissioner Gordon (Pat Hingle) sputters into his radio: "What are you waiting for? The Signal!"

And then, illuminated in the Gotham night sky, is the renowned Bat-Signal. Moments later, a swift, powerful jet-black vehicle ploughs it way into the Plaza and to the city's rescue. It's the Batmobile...and inside its jet-like cockpit is the Dark Knight...Batman (Michael Keaton)!

The attack on Gotham Plaza would take a full three weeks to film, shot by the first *and* second unit companies. Max Kleven – who in addition to his stunt coordinating duties also functioned with Billy Weber as second unit director – would bring a number of stunt "firsts" to *Batman Returns*. "Tim Burton is the kind of director who allows you to experiment," says Kleven, a tall, strong, silent type who believes that actions should speak louder than words.

One of the most elaborate of these experiments undertaken by Kleven and Charlie Croughwell (co-stunt coordinator) involved ground-breaking work with a fairly old but trusted technique, known in the stunt world as "ratcheting."

Explains Croughwell – a tough, wiry Irish-American whose work on *Batman Returns* included a 45-foot plunge while doubling on stunt duties – "A ratchet is a huge pneumatic cylinder which looks like a big shock absorber. When it's filled with compressed air and triggered, the ratchet will catapult the stuntman attached to it with cables in any direction you rig him for."

What made the ratcheting work on *Batman Returns* so special was threefold: the sheer number of people who were ratcheted at the same time; the fact that it wasn't only *people* who were ratcheted; Kleven and Croughwell utilized a system newly advanced by stuntman/stunt-innovator Brian Smrz which actually allows the ratchet operators to *decelerate* the stuntplayer in mid-flight by carefully releasing the air through different valves, allowing him to hit pin-pointed targets rather than just go off like an unguided missile.

When the giant Christmas present blows open, five Red Triangle Circus Gang goons – all stuntmen, of course – are blasted out at once. Six cameras covered the moment from every conceivable angle, as the stuntmen were guided to their destinations by the decelerating ratchets and their own tremendous skills.

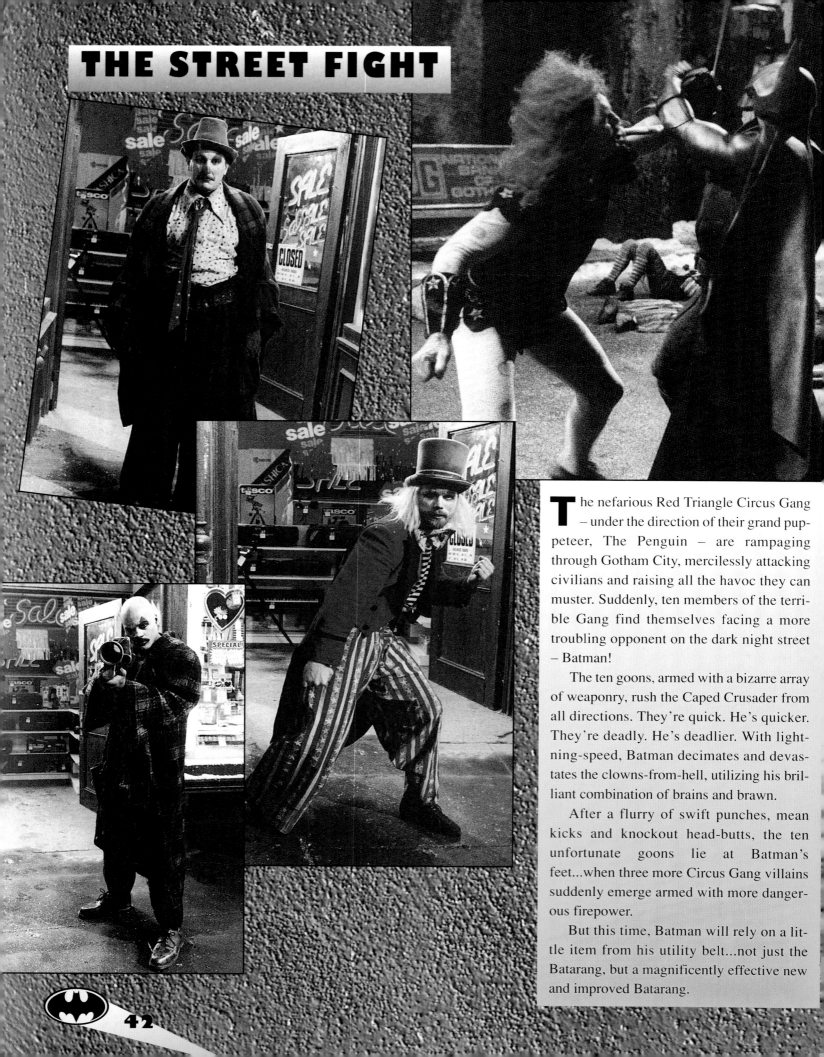

THE STREET FIGHT

The nefarious Red Triangle Circus Gang – under the direction of their grand puppeteer, The Penguin – are rampaging through Gotham City, mercilessly attacking civilians and raising all the havoc they can muster. Suddenly, ten members of the terrible Gang find themselves facing a more troubling opponent on the dark night street – Batman!

The ten goons, armed with a bizarre array of weaponry, rush the Caped Crusader from all directions. They're quick. He's quicker. They're deadly. He's deadlier. With lightning-speed, Batman decimates and devastates the clowns-from-hell, utilizing his brilliant combination of brains and brawn.

After a flurry of swift punches, mean kicks and knockout head-butts, the ten unfortunate goons lie at Batman's feet...when three more Circus Gang villains suddenly emerge armed with more dangerous firepower.

But this time, Batman will rely on a little item from his utility belt...not just the Batarang, but a magnificently effective new and improved Batarang.

BEHIND THE ACTION

"There's a guy named Benny Urquidez," says Max Kleven, "an undefeated kick-boxing champion who runs a gym in North Hollywood. We asked Benny to sift through the guys who go to his gym, select ten of the toughest fighters he could find, and show up with that gang to fight Batman."

Deciding to load *Batman Returns* with three times more action than the first film, Tim Burton wanted a scene which showcases the Dark Knight's physical prowess, emphasizing the fact that since Batman is a superhero without super powers he has to fight *mano-a-mano* like everyone else.

"You're seeing the best there is in Hollywood in this scene," promises Kleven. Adds Charlie Croughwell, "the fight choreography is a combination of beautiful martial arts combined with pure street fighting."

Dave Lea, the British-born, cockney-accented kickboxing champ who trained Michael Keaton for both films, further explains: "Now, what Batman's got is ten guys, not coming at him one-at-a-time, but all-at-once. In this particular fight, no one's standing still. Batman and the circus goons are just ripping into each other." Lea hastens to add, however, that although the fight is tremendously exciting, "it's more fun than brutal to watch. It isn't so violent that kids wouldn't enjoy the action and movement."

Michael Keaton enjoyed filming the sequence, which was shot over three chilly nights. Carefully following the fight choreography, Keaton looked fast and furious as the battling Batman...sometimes breaking up the tension (and the crew as well) with even faster and more furious jokes. Urquidez's tougher-than-leather fighters/goons couldn't staunch their laughter, which made them look a *lot* more friendly!

43

BATMAN AND CATWOMAN'S ROOFTOP TANGLE

Gotham City's new menace – a beautiful, slinky and absolutely ferocious force of nature known as Catwoman (Michelle Pfeiffer) – has just nonchalantly blown the blazes out of Max Shreck's (Christopher Walken) elaborate department store.

Batman chases her up to the rooftops high above the fiery cataclysm, and finds Catwoman curled up like a...well...pussycat. Suddenly, she fires off a furious flurry of kicks, punches and swipes to Batman's face, and he returns the favor in kind with a wallop that sends her cringing into a whimpering ball.

"How could you?" she sniffs at Batman. "I'm a woman!"

The Caped Crusader is aghast at his own cruelty toward one so weak and delicate. "I'm...sorry...I..." he says as he approaches her. Imagine Batman's surprise as Catwoman uncoils and delivers a well-placed boot to his nether regions, knocking him over the edge of the building.

Suddenly, Catwoman lashes out with her bullwhip, expertly wrapping it around Batman's arm. Jerking him up, she ties the other end of her whip to a weather vane. "As I was saying," she tells Batman pointedly, "I'm a woman, and can't be taken for granted. Are you listening, you Batman you?"

"Hanging on every word," the helpless man responds.

"Good joke," she ripostes. "Wanna hear another one?" Batman nods in assent (he has but little choice).

"The world tells boys to conquer the world, and girls to wear clean panties," declares Catwoman. "A man dressed as a bat is a he-man, but a woman dressed as a cat is a she-devil. I'm just living down to my expectations. Life's a bitch...now, so am I!"

Batman may be all tied up, but he's not yet down for the count. This is just the beginning of a very special relationship between the Dark Knight and his equally divided antagonist.

BEHIND THE ACTION

Believe it or not," says Michelle Pfeiffer, "the physical work has been the easiest part of playing Catwoman for me. I did so much training before we started shooting, and I had great fighting and whip trainers."

Talk about a work ethic! For her role of Catwoman, Michelle Pfeiffer worked several hours each week, months before the cameras started to roll, first with kickboxer Kathy Long on her fighting technique, then with Anthony De Longis on her whip skills. By the time she was ready to shoot, Pfeiffer could kickbox with the best of them, and as for her whip-wielding eloquence: "Michelle is kicking butt," says De Longis, who is not only an expert with the whip, but a black belt in Tae Kwon Do and a ranked sabre fencer who's taught stage combat and character movement in the UCLA Theatre Arts department for over 15 years.

"I know of only one or two other people who have made this a major hobby who have anything like Michelle's vocabulary with the whip," continues De Longis. "She's an actress with a tremendous amount of emotional impact. Michelle has been utilizing that whip as a dynamic point of connection...she takes her energy and channels it into the whip."

"Michael and Michelle are both doing their own stuff on that rooftop," confirms Max Kleven, "and it's pretty unusual for two stars to do so much physical work."

"Michael never got fed up or frustrated with his training," says Dave Lea, "because it was always something new and enjoyable. The rooftop fight was the first major battle between Batman and Catwoman, so we really had to make it dramatic and strong. For me, to see Michael and Michelle working so hard was really astounding."

THE BATMOBILE'S HELL-RIDE

Framed by The Penguin (Danny DeVito) to look like he sent the Ice Princess (Cristi Conaway) plunging to her doom, Batman is trying to escape pursuing police cars in his Batmobile when an ignominious face appears on the vehicle's console screen.

"Don't adjust your set," squawks The Penguin. "Welcome to the Oswald Cobblepot School of Driving. Gentlemen, start your screaming!"

Batman realizes, to his horror, that the Batmobile has been tampered with and is now controlled by his vengeful nemesis. Indeed, The Penguin is sitting in the driver's seat of a miniature kiddie-ride version of the Batmobile, commanding the *real* Batmobile on the terrifying drive of its life.

As the Batmobile thunders forward, careering wildly through the streets of Gotham, The Penguin informs the Caped Crusader, "Maybe this is a bad time to mention it, but my license has expired...of course, so have you!"

The Batmobile rushes toward a major traffic jam on a one-way street, with The Penguin still having a hellish field day at the controls. There's no way to stop it! The Batmobile ploughs through almost 20 cars, blasting them in all directions. They twirl through the air, strike fire hydrants and huge metal pipes, sparks and flames everywhere as terrified pedestrians run in all directions to escape the carnage.

BEHIND THE ACTION

Once again, it was ratchet time on the Warner Bros. backlot, where a mammoth outdoor "down-town Gotham City" set had been constructed. "We'd had such good luck ratcheting people," Max Kleven notes with a smile, "that we said, 'Well, let's try to ratchet some cars!'"

Okay, simple enough, right? Wrong. Because at no time in the history of stunt cinema had anyone ever attempted to ratchet cars and control their movements. "I've done primitive versions of this before," recalls Kleven, "but only with one or two vehicles." This time, they had to simultaneously ratchet 13 full-sized cars – another record!

A tough job required a tough guy to handle it, so Kleven asked Charlie Croughwell to be at the controls of the Batmobile when it plummeted down the street. "When the Batmobile was about six, seven feet away from the back end of the cars, we would ratchet them over in conjunction with an explosion set up on each car, which to several cameras covering the scene made it look like the Batmobile was actually smashing into them."

In fact, Croughwell never impacted any of the other vehicles. "I would swerve the Batmobile to make it look to the camera like I was hitting the cars. But I didn't really hit those cars at all."

Obviously, a scene of this size and complexity required tremendous coordination between departments. "There was a person on each ratchet handling each of the 13 cars," remarks Kleven. "So when the Batmobile got to a certain point, it was time for them to press the button. In the meantime, the mechanical effects guys were taking care of the explosions."

Oh yes, one more little detail. Inside each one of those 13 unfortunate vehicles was a stuntplayer, to give the sequence a totally realistic aspect. And absolutely no one was even scratched when the smoke cleared!

The Penguin CRASHES The Party

Bruce Wayne (Michael Keaton) and Selina Kyle (Michelle Pfeiffer) are enjoying a romantic dance at Max Shreck's opulent Christmas time Maxsquerade Ball. Surrounded by weirdly masked members of Gotham City's upper crust, the two divided souls try to forget their travails in a soulful spin on the glass dance floor...

...Which suddenly, shatteringly explodes from beneath, hurling dancers through the air, projecting broken glass in all directions. And rising through the smoke is a giant yellow Duck Vehicle, manned by The Penguin (Danny DeVito) and several of his armed-to-the-beaks Penguin Commandos.

"You didn't invite me," The Penguin bellows, "so I crashed!"

Bruce and Selina slip away in the confusion, while The Penguin takes Max Shreck hostage, spiriting him down below Gotham in his mobile Duck.

BEHIND THE ACTION

There are two huge explosions in *Batman Returns* which we had to accomplish on soundstages," notes mechanical effects wizard Chuck Gaspar. "When Catwoman blows up Shreck's Department Store, and when the dance floor explodes at the Maxsquerade Ball. Only the dance floor explosion was a lot more challenging, because we had real people standing right on top of it!"

"The only way this scene would really work," continues mechanical effects foreman Mike Edmonson, "is if it looked like the floor itself drove the people up into the air. So the stunt people had a great idea...let's get as many people in there as we can, hook 'em up to ratchets and cables, and yank them into the air when the floor goes up!"

Tim Burton decided that 14 lucky stunt-people would get ratcheted in the middle of these massive shockwaves. And there you have yet another record – it's the most num-

ber of people ever ratcheted at one time.

Brian Smrz and his associate, Scott Sproule, rehearsed with the ratchets and stuntplayers for about a week, making sure that the timing would be exactly right. "They worked it out and did a beautiful job," notes Chuck Gaspar. "But we didn't get a chance to rehearse the floor. You can only blow it up once! We had to have it right on the first take, because it was a very expensive shot to think about re-doing."

"We used half-inch tempered glass for the dance floor," continues Mike Edmonson, "which would easily support the stuntplayer/dancers' weight. Then, about six feet underneath them, we placed about eight 20 inch x 20 inch conical mortars, filled with broken tempered glass. Then we had a couple of black powder bombs to create a little bit of smoke in the area after the floor goes up."

Choosing to be right on the battlefield, Max Kleven and Charlie Croughwell donned appropriate tuxedos and oversaw the entire effect as stuntplayers. "On film it all looks like it goes up at once," says Croughwell. "But actually, the ratchets took the people up just a beat before the floor blew up."

"Right," confirms Edmonson. "When they hit a point where they were starting to be jerked off the floor, then it was time for us to push the button, which I took the responsibility for."

Fortunately for everybody, the timing was absolutely perfect. The shot went off like a dream. The stuntplayers on the ratchets flew into the air, bounced off walls, furniture, railings. Sixty extra stuntpeople in key positions fell to the ground as broken glass blasted all around them. In the final film, none of those ratchet cables will be visible. And when the smoke cleared, everyone – including a very happy Tim Burton – took a look at the replay on video and felt that they had all done a decent day's work.

From concept to lighting to cinematic reality, the old Gotham Cemetery was first sketched by art department illustrator Marty Kline (top), then meticulously lit by cinematographer Stefan Czapsky (main), and preserved for the ages with the scene of The Penguin visiting the grave of his unfaithful parents (right). Above: Boss Films, one of the special effects companies contributing to the film, prepares an elaborate shot at Shreck's Department Store.

BEHIND The Scenes

In movieland lingo, "above-the-line" refers to the major, big-time participants in the production of a film: the producers, the director, the screenwriters, the stars. "Below-the-line" refers to the core of production personnel – like grips, gaffers, wardrobe, make-up, cameramen – the rough-talking, hard-walking folks who get the physical job done.

> **"I view my job as the horse pulling the cart. I've worked on low-budget movies and big-budget movies, but basically the job at hand is exactly the same -- get the film made the way the director wants it made!"**
>
> LARRY FRANCO, CO-PRODUCER

CO-PRODUCER

LARRY FRANCO

One of Hollywood's most respected production experts, *Batman Returns* co-producer Larry Franco would be the first to admit he's an above-the-line guy with a below-the-line heart. "I grew up in a small town," asserts Franco, "and I'd like to think that I still have small town values. I'm a line producer, which means I'm riding right on the line. And I feel a very strong affinity to the people who are below-the-line."

The bearded, Northern California born-and-bred Franco was a constant presence on the set, often wearing his coveted San Francisco 49ers football team jacket and fielding any and all problems like a stalwart quarterback.

And if Larry Franco sounds like he knows what he's talking about, he does. As an assistant director in the late 1970s, Franco paid his dues by spending almost a year in the hellish jungles of the Philippines with Francis Ford Coppola, a survivor of the entire, legendary *Apocalypse Now* (1979) shoot. Franco then forged a 10-year professional relationship with director John

Carpenter, producing such films of the imagination as *Escape From New York* (1981), *Christine* (1983), *Starman* (1984) and *Big Trouble in Little China* (1986). After co-producing the hit action film *Tango & Cash* (1989), Franco went on to serve as the executive producer of Walt Disney Studios' big-scale fantasy *The Rocketeer* (1991).

"I'm a nuts-and-bolts producer more than anything else," avows Franco. "It's my job to take a script and get it on the screen. Physically. Mechanically. Logistically. And when I see my name on the screen, or on the poster...well, that's enough for me."

ASSOCIATE PRODUCER/ UNIT PRODUCTION MANAGER

IAN BRYCE

Ian Bryce knows his way around a big-time movie set. This is a man, after all, who worked as a second assistant director on *Return of the Jedi* (1983) and *Indiana Jones and the Temple of Doom* (1984); production executive on *Willow* (1988); associate producer of TV's *Ewoks: The Battle for Endor* (1986); and unit production manager on *Tucker: The Man and His Dream* (1988), *Indiana Jones and the Last Crusade* (1989) and, most recently, *The Rocketeer*.

On *Batman Returns*, this native of Totnes,

England was charged with the responsibility of supervising the day-to-day operation of the film, overseeing the work of more than 200 first-unit crew, about 125 second-unit crew, and more than 700 others who were working on various aspects of the movie.

"The logistics of a film like *Batman Returns* are immense," admits Bryce, "but we've had the luxury of hiring top-notch people in all departments. Everyone from our production coordinator to our accountant, and those who work for them, are absolutely super. I couldn't do this job without them."

Bryce was the linchpin in the production office base camp, staffed by the several dedicated, intelligent and utterly independent women, self dubbed the "Bat Babes". Even the department bicycle, used as transportation around the huge Warner Bros. backlot, was emblazoned with the "Bat Babes" logo.

In the middle of all this cyclonic activity was Bryce, meticulously attending to every detail of production, no matter how monumental or minute. "One of the things that I like about being a production manager is that you're immersed in the center of everything," he declares. "Yeah, I love it. I don't know what else I would do that could be more fun!"

THE SCREENWRITERS

DANIEL WATERS & WESLEY STRICK

"When you're working on a Tim Burton movie", says Daniel Waters, "you're dealing with a completely alternative reality. You're given the freedom to do just about anything. You can't be too operatic, too baroque, too unusual. The only rule going into *Batman Returns* was that there were no rules."

Waters is a soft-spoken man who is best known as the author of *Heathers* (1989), starring Winona Ryder and Christian Slater. That unforgettable, unsparing view of the denizens of an American high school was produced by

Denise Di Novi. The writer discovered that he and Tim Burton "work very well in a yin/yang sense. Visually, Tim puts no limits on himself and I try not to put any limits on myself when it comes to ideas and words."

What Waters set out to do in *Batman Returns* was to create a vast canvas on which larger-than-life characters play out their individual and collective dramas of revenge, redemption and romance. For example, notes Waters, "Catwoman starts off like your typical harassed secretary...but then transcends into something incredibly powerful and complex. Batman, The Penguin, Catwoman, Max Shreck, these characters all have magnificent fates much exaggerated from the rest of us."

Making his own unique contributions to *Batman Returns* was Wesley Strick, one of Hollywood's most sought-after screenwriters (and now a director, having started his first such assignment, *Pure Heart*, after completing his work on *Batman Returns*). Most recently, Strick was responsible for two tense psychological thrillers: *Cape Fear* (1991) and *Final Analysis* (1992).

Opposite top: Co-producer extraordinaire Larry Franco. Opposite bottom: Detail-oriented associate producer/production manager Ian Bryce. Above: Screenwriters Daniel Waters (right) and Wesley Strick (left) infused their youth, passion and creative impertinence into a highly original and often outrageous script.

> **"There was a very conscious effort not to make either The Penguin or Catwoman just villains incarnate. I wanted to give pathos to both characters, a real depth of feeling so that we can understand their evil deeds. This makes them much more interesting, even poignant."**
> **DANIEL WATERS, SCREENWRITER**

"To me, *Batman Returns* has two strong stories, which hopefully function well together," notes Strick. "There's Batman versus The Penguin...and then there's the whole Batman/Catwoman/Bruce/Selina story. The whole subplot approaches issues of sex and desire and love and romance in ways that I think are very rich. So it sort of rounds out for me the new Batman myth that was started in the first movie. It adds a whole subtext of feeling, and humor too."

"This is one of the few chances that exist for a screenwriter to work with things that are so much larger than life," concludes Daniel Waters. "You can bring in anything. You can't go too far with this movie, because we're starting out at such a wild, anything-goes level."

Artist, Czapsky would have to start writing his acceptance speech, which would probably consist of an embarrassed "thank you" and nothing more.

The formidable task of translating Tim Burton's challenging visual concepts for *Batman Returns* onto film fell to the affable, bear-like Czapsky, who had previously collaborated with the director on *Edward Scissorhands*. Director and cinematographer created an almost shorthand communication. Somehow, everything was understood. Burton and Czapsky speak each other's language, which requires *very* few words.

From the muted tones of the Batcave and the dark night streets of Gotham City to the explosive colors of the Maxsquerade Ball and the Yuletide attack on Gotham Plaza, Czapsky had to strike the perfect aesthetic balance. And like Tim Burton, Czapsky would rather paint pictures on film than endlessly talk about what he does for a living. "I just try to listen to the director and satisfy his needs for what is best for the movie," says the cinematographer simply.

In fact, Czapsky is considered one of the most imaginative young directors of photography to burst upon the screen in recent years. Born in Oesterscheppes, West Germany, he emigrated to Cleveland, Ohio with his Ukrainian parents while still an infant. After studying film at New York's Columbia University, Czapsky began working for more than a decade in the blue-collar end of filmmaking: as a grip, gaffer and assistant cameraman.

Since graduating to full cinematographer status in 1985, Czapsky has photographed such films as *The Thin Blue Line* (1988), *Last Exit to Brooklyn* (1989), *The Dark Wind* (1992) and *Prelude to a Kiss* (1992), in addition to his celebrated films with Tim Burton.

"I try not to be too intellectual about film," Czapsky maintains. "For me, film is simply an emotional and visual experience."

DIRECTOR OF PHOTOGRAPHY

STEFAN CZAPSKY

Stefan Czapsky is just like the guy next door, if the guy next door happened to be one of the world's finest cinematographers. If Oscars were handed out for Least Pretentious

THE COMPOSER

DANNY ELFMAN

Thunderous and heroic, sweeping and romantic, Gothic and eerie, heart-stirring and soul-pounding, Danny Elfman's music for *Batman* presented a perfect aural backdrop for Tim Burton's memorable images.

In fact, Danny Elfman always presents a perfect aural backdrop for Tim Burton's memorable images, since he has been the composer for all five of that director's feature films – *Pee-wee's Big Adventure*, *Beetlejuice*, *Batman*, *Edward Scissorhands* and now *Batman Returns*. This symbiotic union of sight and sound has produced one of the most fruitful director/composer collaborations since Alfred Hitchcock and Bernard Herrmann.

Like Batman, Elfman leads a double life: one, as a founding member of Oingo Boingo, playing energetic, witty and individualistic rock and roll for more than a decade; the other, as one of the movie world's most versatile and successful composers.

In addition to Burton's films, Elfman has scored *Big Top Pee-wee* (1988), *Scrooged* (1988), *Midnight Run* (1988), *Nightbreed* (1990), *Darkman* (1990) and *Dick Tracy* (1990), among others. He's also written themes for the popular TV programs "Pee-wee's Playhouse", "Tales From The Crypt", "The Flash" and "The Simpsons". A compilation of film and television music from this oftime Grammy nominee – "Music For A Darkened Theatre" – was released in 1991 on the MCA label.

During one of his visits to the *Batman Returns* set, Elfman enthusiastically joined in with the rest of the crew, who were recruited to toss a nasty salad of fruits and vegetables at Danny DeVito's Penguin for a crucial scene of the movie. "I also hurled water on the *Darkman* set," noted the puckish Elfman.

Could this be yet another trend started by the immensely innovative Danny Elfman?

Opposite: Director of photography Stefan Czapsky, a master of light and shadow. Left: Innovative composer Danny Elfman who was an active off-camera pitcher of eggs, tomatoes and cabbages when the citizens of Gotham City finally give The Penguin his proper due.

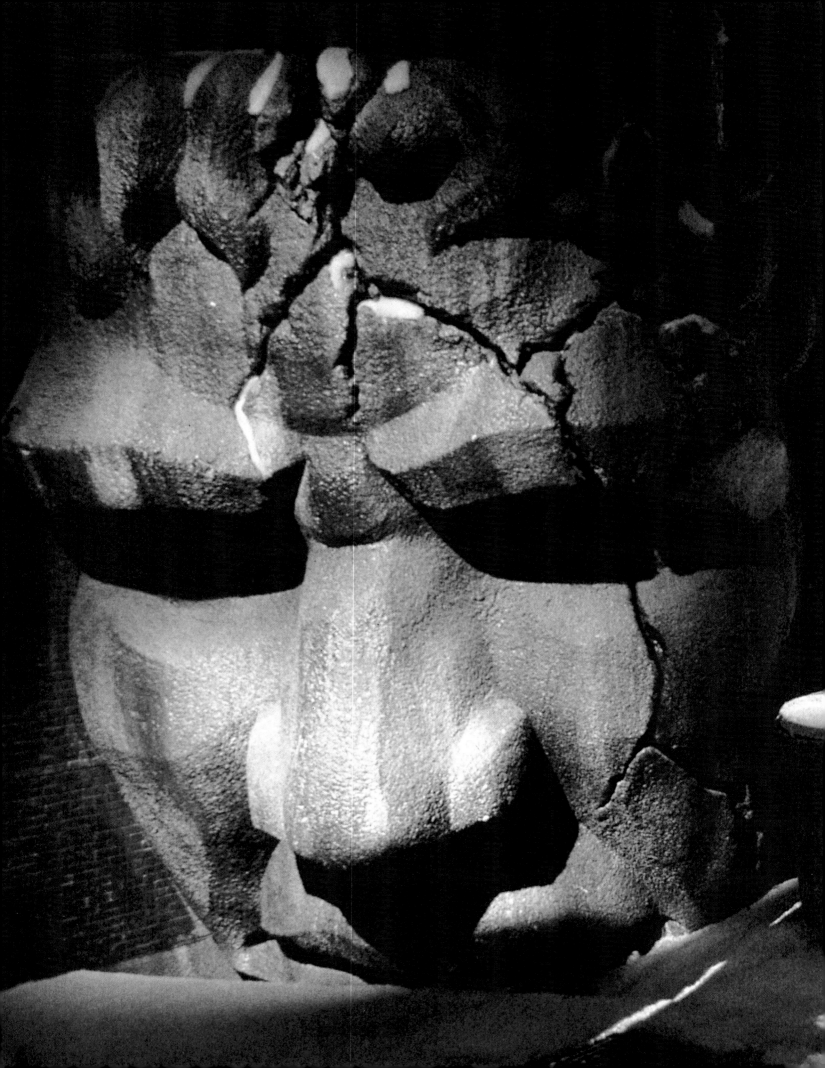

PRODUCTION DESIGN

An empty motion picture soundstage is a ghostly, eerie environment. Half-perceived shadows seem to lurk in the corners. The smallest whispers echo in the vastness.

But to those unusual movieland personages called production designers, an empty motion picture soundstage isn't barren at all. For every vacant space, they can see wonders forming in their mind's eye. The ghosts vanish, to be replaced by whatever their talents can create.

Imagine what went through Bo Welch's head when he looked at seven empty playgrounds (that is, soundstages) at Warner Bros. and another at Universal. The results, even while *Batman Returns* was still being filmed, became legendary in the Hollywood community. Not just for their size and scope – gigantic sets have been seen since the days of the silents – but for a remarkable fusion of grandeur and wit that was utterly appropriate for the film being made by Tim Burton.

"We didn't set out to design an amusement park," states Bo Welch in his office, surrounded by sketches, illustrations, models and other brick-a-brack. "First and foremost, the sets had to function as a backdrop to the action rather than exist for their own sake."

Bo Welch (above) created a massive and witty Gotham City, including a crumbling, half-buried Greco-Roman bust (opposite) and a huge, bizarre cathedral, shown under construction (above).

The task facing Bo Welch was considerable: redesign Gotham City in alignment with Tim Burton's revised vision of Batman and the world he inhabits, along with a plethora of props, weaponry and vehicles.

Understandably, this turned out to be a long and highly collaborative process. Welch worked closely with his brilliant art directors, Tom Duffield and Rick Heinrichs, set decorator Cheryl Carasik, prop masters Bill and Vic Petrotta, and their attendant staffs of talented production illustrators, storyboard artists, model makers and set designers. Not to mention a construction crew which numbered more than 300 people – the artisans, carpenters, molders and painters who really built Gotham City – under the supervision of construction coordinator Greg Callas and general foreman Richard Hoffenberg.

"Hollywood has the most organized filmmaking system in the world," says Rick Heinrichs, "and with *Batman Returns* we wanted to take full advantage of that organization." With such a vibrantly creative staff, Bo Welch gladly accepted any and all contributions which would work for the film. "Only a fool would reject good ideas because they didn't come from himself," he declares.

Welch, whose previous credits include *Beetlejuice* and *Edward Scissorhands*, as well

Art department illustrator Tom Lay painted these beautifully detailed pre-production conceptions of Gotham Plaza under bat attack (top), the Shreck Industries conference room (middle) and the lofty rooftops of Gotham (above).

as *Ghostbusters II* (1989) and *Grand Canyon* (1991), is a casual but ferociously determined soul whose relentlessly dry sense of humor snaked its way into almost every situation, including the movie's overall design.

While a wide range of architectural and design influences can be detected in Welch's Gotham City (which set decorator Cheryl Carasik defines as "Machine Age Teutonic"), the results are wholly original and singular.

"Overall, what we wanted to do in the design of *Batman Returns*, was to create the impression of 'city,'" maintains Welch. "You never see any set or any piece of this movie in its entirety. You see a piece of the city here and another piece there. It allows your mind to fill in the rest and use your own imagination."

GOTHAM PLAZA

One of the largest interior sets ever built at Warner Bros., the 65-foot tall Gotham Plaza is, according to Welch, "a deliberate caricature of Rockefeller Center in New York — something like its weirder twin. The design is clearly influenced by fascist and totalitarian architecture and statuary, dehumanizing in its scale, with hints of the other parts of the city peeking into the corners."

Among the Plaza's more unique elements are several statues, superbly sculpted by Leo Rijn and his crew. They include two colossi setting the grinding gears of Gotham City in motion; four startling fascistic statues surrounding the 35-foot tall Christmas tree, given the monikers "Misery, Grief, Ecstasy and Victory" by Bo Welch ("which actually refers to my work process," he quipped); and a large stone Greco-Roman head, half-buried in the pavement due to Gotham City's propensity for building one layer on top of an older one.

Ringed by Shreck's Department Store,

Left: A batallion of cranes and construction workers were required for the two months-plus building of Gotham Plaza on Stage 16, which is the largest such structure at Warner Bros. Studios.
Above: One of the four stylized figures lending Gotham Plaza its decidedly totalitarian aspect, designed by Bo Welch and sculpted from a foam foundation by Leo Rijn.

looming government buildings and one tottering skyscraper, Gotham Plaza "isn't so much mean and evil as it is inhospitable and demoralizing," asserts Welch. "The buildings are meant to dwarf the human beings down below. But when you see the citizens of Gotham gather in this Plaza with their shopping bags and their families, you get the feeling that despite the surroundings, you cannot repress the human spirit."

THE PENGUIN'S LAIR

A wonderland for the live penguins who acted in many of the scenes shot within, The Penguin's Lair was a magnificent but undeniably creepy environment for the human cast and crew.

Built inside a soundstage with a 50-foot ceiling at Universal Studios (since the biggest Warner stage was already occupied by Gotham Plaza), the Lair is the old, crumbling, abandoned aquatic pavilion (part of the old, crumbling, abandoned Gotham Zoo) where The Penguin is raised from infancy. It's the villain's true home.

"In designing the set," explains Welch, "we researched theme parks, old World's Fair aquariums, synchronized swimming shows, and man-made animal habitats. You let all that stuff fester inside of your brain...then you take those impressions and feelings, and try to enhance and magnify them.

"You think of what would happen to one of those old places if 50 years had gone by. It's rotting, spooky, with green moss crawling up the sides of the walls. What was a beautiful kind of white, light arctic display has now become a dangerous petri dish for The Penguin and his army to grow in."

The moat that separates the grandstand from the pavilion performance area required 25,000 gallons of water to keep filled. And that huge, rusted, wheezing, bobbing air conditioner that keeps The Penguin cool was

Top and above: Two more of Marty Kline's pre-production illustrations, envisioning the expo-architecture of the Arctic World pavilion and the subterranean glories of the Batcave. Main: The Penguin's Lair in all of its creepy, crawly vastness, built full-size with 50-foot-tall ceilings and 25,000 gallons of ice-cold and rather slimy water.

only a prop. Modern, high-tech air condition-
ers kept the temperatures inside the Lair down
to about 40 degrees Fahrenheit. Great for arctic birds, a little chilly for people, especially
those crew members who spent much of the
shooting day in the water, with hip waders
their only protection from the big chill.

THE BATCAVE

Like every set in the movie, the Batcave is
brand new and unlike anything that's been
seen before. "We basically have the same set
of guidelines as the traditional Batcave,"
remarks Welch. "It's dark and dangerous and
endless, but also with a certain amount of
safety and enclosure."

The massive set filled the soundstage, its
two largest sections housing the Batmobile
(and its gleaming metal fuel tanks) on one end
and the Batcave consoles – one for Batman
and the other for Alfred – on the other. There's
a ring of blue runway landing lights on the
perimeter of the precipice, to prevent Batman
and Alfred from tumbling over the edge and
into the endless abyss of the cave.

**Above: With forced
perspective skyscrapers
as a dramatic backdrop,
Gotham Plaza's imposing
sculptures dominate the
square with their severe,
fascistic countenances.
The gear-pulling colos-
sus, engulfed in steam, is
a particularly frightening
vision of mass control.**

A large holding space for Batman's armored suits is separated from the main lab and accessible only by a medieval-style drawbridge. The rows of costumes within look like an imposing army of Batmen!

As for the laboratory consoles, they're organically built into the black slate rock and are, according to Welch, "multi-tech", a mixture of old and new video and audio devices, tracking screens, surveillance equipment, revolving radar, and, most humorously in the case of Alfred's console, an ironing board, sink and refrigerator for his less technical and more domestic tasks.

GOTHAM ROOFTOPS

Two combined Warner Bros. soundstages held the length and breadth of the spectacular Gotham City "rooftops" set, the staging ground for much action sequences high above the city, particularly the very physical battles-of-the-sexes between Batman and Catwoman.

"Rooftops exude a kind of romantic feeling to me," muses Welch. "The irony about big cities is that they often look the most beautiful from rooftops. You can see the lights of other windows, interesting silhouettes, the best decorations, spectacular cityscapes. There's always a kind of mystery, and a lot more air than the claustrophobic streets below."

This set features some of Welch's most interesting designs, an entire city built to scale and forced perspective. Huge, looming

stone faces – a motif in Welch's Gotham City – peer down upon the tiny inhabitants below. Up on the roofs, air circulator fans whir and smokestacks belch steam. Set decorator Carasik provided suitably small-scale Christmas wreaths and lights for the little windows off in the distance. All in all, absolutely magical.

WAYNE MANOR & STUFFY MANSION

Batman Returns features not one, but two huge mansion interiors – Wayne Manor and the so-called "Stuffy Mansion." Wayne Manor, of course, houses Bruce Wayne, the respectable philanthropist whose secret double life reveals him as the Dark Knight of Gotham City. The "Stuffy Mansion" is the pristine home of Tucker and Esther Cobblepot, parents of baby Oswald, better known as The Penguin.

"In terms of size and scale, Wayne Manor is colossal," admits the production designer. "Wayne Manor is the *essence* of mansion. And to me, mansion means big and extravagant, whether in finishing or furnishings. The size is very important, because the audience needs to have a sense of this lonely man, Bruce Wayne, rattling around in this tremendous house that he inherited with Alfred as his only companion."

Wayne Manor is overwhelmingly huge and heroic, its Gothic designs accentuated with beautifully-detailed dark wood and exquisitely carved, heavy furniture. Special features of Wayne Manor include a 27-foot tall reproduction of Raphael's "St. Michael" (a gigantic winged figure who is half-angel, half-avenger), the tremendous "two car" fireplace, a library containing thousands of beautifully-bound old books. In the library is a frightening, medieval Iron Maiden which actually functions as Batman's quick route to the Batcave.

As a contrast to Wayne Manor, the

The Penguin hard at work (right) in the twisted, decrepit upstairs portion of the Cobblepot for Mayor headquarters (below), located on a busy, snowswept Gotham City thoroughfare entirely created inside of Warner Bros.' Stage 25.

Opposite top: Selina Kyle's typical "working girl" apartment, with steel beam projecting right through the kitchen. By contrast (opposite middle) the enormous interior of Wayne Manor, including a Gothic tropical fish tank (opposite bottom) containing a scale model replica of the manor.

"Stuffy Mansion" is "white, gold, frilly, overbearing to the point of irritation," according to Welch. "The oppressive architectural detail and set dressing will hopefully make your skin crawl. The main reasons for the light colors is to act as a contrast to the black steel playpen cage that the Penguin boy is kept inside of – your focus should be on this mysterious baby manbeast inside of this black armored box, set against a rich white and gold backdrop."

THE PENGUIN'S CAMPAIGN HEADQUARTERS

The very first scenes to be filmed for *Batman Returns* were shot on this impressive set,

which is adjoined by Gotham streets, alleyways and buildings.

The building from which Oswald Cobblepot (aka The Penguin) launches his mayoral campaign is a classic big city structure, with pounded tin ceilings and rounded pillars. Downstairs, in the actual campaign office, clean-cut workers toil in an atmosphere of immaculate antiseptic whiter-than-whiteness.

Climb the metal winding staircase upstairs, however, and you find the evil and malignant twin of the lower floor – the same layout and architecture, but rotting, rusted, the pillars caving in at crazy angles, venetian blinds askew, a feeble air conditioner cooling The Penguin and his Red Triangle Circus Gang henchmen as they plot Gotham City's destruction.

Ingeniously, The Penguin's Campaign Headquarters would later be converted into the Hall of Records, where The Penguin searches (or so we think) for information about his long-lost parents. And the upstairs quarters would be transformed by Welch and company into a loft where Batman and Catwoman battle it out, cape and claw.

COSTUMES

For The Penguin and Catwoman, Bob Ringwood and Mary Vogt had to create designs that were essentially faithful to the popular concepts of the long-established characters, while blazing paths that would newly personify them on film.

Above: Costume designers Bob Ringwood and Mary Vogt, a cross-Atlantic visionary alliance. Top right: Batman's "wardrobe," accessible only by a drawbridge.

Building the Better Batman. That was the primary reason why Tim Burton agreed to direct *Batman Returns* and this philosophy extended to every facet of the production. Nothing would be exactly the way it was in the first *Batman* movie, including Batman's costume.

No one could have been more up to the task of creating the thousands of costumes for *Batman Returns* than Bob Ringwood, the enthusiastic Englishman who served as costume designer for the 1989 film. And due to the sheer volume of work on the second movie, Ringwood was joined by an American costume designer, the talented Mary Vogt.

For *Batman Returns*, Ringwood and Vogt not only had to create a new Batman costume for the Caped Crusader and appropriate dress for The Penguin and Catwoman; they also had to come up with clothes for a cast of thousands, including residents of Gotham City, and the fantastically attired members of the Red Triangle Circus Gang.

CAPED CRUSADER: To begin with, Tim Burton required a modification of the first movie's Batman costume, which was itself a dramatic alteration of the comic book's familiar blue-and-gray tights. The filmmaker felt that it had already become overly familiar, and required a re-thinking, while remaining true to the essence of the previous film's costume.

"The fact is that Batman's new costume is much closer to the original concept we had for the first film," says Ringwood, surrounded by his creations in the rangy *Batman Returns* costume shop. "It's more like armor now, rather than a muscle suit. We've also modified the mask by strengthening the eyebrows and the nose, and changing the shape of the eyes and chin."

The right word for the new Batman costume is "streamlined," directly relating to the popular Art Deco style of the 1920s and 1930s that affected architecture and all aspects of interior and industrial design. Vin Burnham was the supervisor of the *Batman Returns* Fabrication Shop, affectionately dubbed the "Bat Shop" by those who worked there. An unmarked and highly secretive facility, the "Bat Shop" was coincidentally located on Burton Avenue, just beneath the

landing pattern of Burbank Airport. It was there, unbeknownst to legions of passing automobiles, airplanes and pedestrians, that the costumes and accessories for Batman, The Penguin and Catwoman were developed and manufactured, using methods and material that are still confidential.

"Batman's original costume was already looking somewhat dated," says the British-born Burnham, who worked on the first *Batman* as well. "So Bob and Mary had various ideas which we talked through relating to 'streamlining.' They brought in pictorial reference of anything from Art Deco train locomotives, statues, pencil sharpeners, vacuum cleaners, anything to help us get a different feeling for the new costume." The

result, everyone agreed, was leaner, meaner and cooler, giving Batman an even more powerful look.

For The Penguin and Catwoman, Ringwood and Vogt also had to create designs that were essentially faithful to the popular concepts of the long-established characters, while blazing paths that would newly personify them on film. Tim Burton's unique sketches were utilized by the designers as a foundation for the elaborate results.

"Tim is a very visual director who's involved with everything, including the costumes," declares Mary Vogt. "As an artist, he's able to provide sketches of his basic ideas, and gives you the freedom to take off from there."

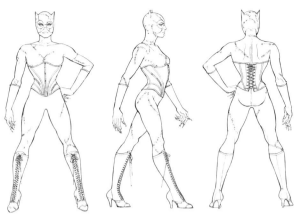

Above: Catwoman's tattered "third stage" costume.
Above right and right: Her provocative "first stage" outfit, sketched and as seen in the film.
Below: The tattooed Snake Woman's outlandish sideshow couture.

SELINA'S SLINKY CAT COSTUME: The only thing more provocative than the re-created Catwoman suit, it was widely agreed, was to see Michelle Pfeiffer actually wearing it! In the story of *Batman Returns*, Selina Kyle makes the costume herself after she's literally brought back from the dead by a coterie of cats. As a result, Catwoman's suit has large, visible white stitches that reveal its home-made origins, becoming more distressed and torn as the film progresses. Those ragged stitches also function as visual suggestions that Selina has been sewn back together again in an act of physical regeneration, not unlike Frankenstein's monster (or, for that matter, Burton's own *Frankenweenie* and *Edward Scissorhands*).

The sleek, shiny, terrifically sexy Catwoman suit was made to fit for Michelle Pfeiffer in every way. Says Ringwood, "When you have someone like Michelle, who's got legs for days, you want to show off those wonderful limbs."

"Catwoman's suit almost looks like liquid on the body," adds Vogt. "It's like she's wearing black glass. And with Michelle in it, the suit looks like a beautiful sort of dark sculpture. We wanted it to be elegant, sexy and modern, very high-tech while still being kind of homey-looking and organic."

THE PENGUIN'S VICTORIAN ELEGANCE: For The Penguin, Ringwood and Vogt not only had to develop the costumes, but also the character's very body shape, which dif-

fers radically from that of Danny DeVito. Again, they looked to Tim Burton's conceptual sketches as a foundation. "We had to create a body and a persona for The Penguin that was in a way repulsive, but also sympathetic," explains Ringwood. "He's an unpleasantly deformed man with penguin-like qualities, like arms that are more like flippers and a roly-poly body."

The costume designers – as well as the hard-working "Bat Shop" crew who would actually create the "body" that Danny DeVito wore underneath his Penguin clothing – were faced with endless technical problems of making all the elements work. "We needed Danny's body suit to move realistically, like real flesh rather than hard rubber," remarks Ringwood. "We also built his shoes in irregular heights, to help Danny walk with that characteristic Penguin waddle."

For the clothes that eventually go on The Penguin's back, Ringwood and Vogt chose a strange, Victorian look that's markedly different from the familiar tuxedo of the comic book. "It's almost like something out of Charles Dickens," declares Ringwood. With

his long, fur-collared coat, satin vest, striped pants, white shirt, Edwardian tie and black top hat, The Penguin does give off a distinct air of Dickensian, tattered elegance.

THE PEOPLE OF GOTHAM CITY: The costumes for the other important characters, from Max Shreck to Alfred, from the Mayor to the Ice Princess – as well as the myriad denizens of Gotham City – depart the Art Deco era for a melange of several periods of American design, creating a sense of time-lessness that is also expressed in Bo Welch's production design. This could be anytime, or no time, a place vaguely remembered from dreams but like no place ever seen before on screen. However, the emphasis was placed on the late 1940s.

"Mary and I both like the late '40s," asserts Ringwood, "especially 1947."

What's so special about 1947? "Following the wartime rationing and deprivations, people really wanted to show off," explains Vogt. "The arts were blooming again, and clothing was very influenced by architecture."

By mixing late 1940s clothing with ele-ments from the '50s, '60s, '70s, '80s and even the '90s, Ringwood and Vogt created a heightened Gotham City style that pushes fashion right to the edge. "If you mix up peri-ods and yet still create a consistent style," smiles Ringwood, "you can bring in almost anything and not be too outrageous."

THE RED TRIANGLE CIRCUS GANG: It was crucial to both Ringwood and Vogt that their costumes be very *American*, albeit in an extremely stylized manner. (The first *Batman* was shot in England, and Ringwood thought that perhaps the costumes were more British in feeling than American. Gotham, after all, is an American city.) However, they drew upon the colorful and somewhat sinis-ter circus traditions of Europe for the Red Triangle Circus Gang costumes, one more outlandish than the other. "Most of the cir-cus stuff really grows out of the late Victorian

period, when the circus was at its height," remarks Ringwood.

Ringwood and Vogt's creations may remind one of the centuries-old *Commedia dell'Arte* tradition, or the Elephant Man-like sideshows of turn-of-the-century England. "The American circus has become very wholesome," says Ringwood. "But the European circus has always been more, shall we say...decadent!"

COSTUME EXTRAVAGANZA: Decadence was also the hallmark of Max Shreck's Christmas-time Maxsquerade Ball, a costume bash to end all costume bashes. For the very unique 182 masks that festoon this sequence, Burton and Ringwood called upon the talents of Ted Shell, whose previous credits include *Star Trek* films one through five, *Gremlins* (1984), *Hook* (1991) and all of the costumes for Michael Jackson's "Victory" tour.

"We wanted to make the Maxsquerade costumes not only fun and fantasy, but also a little bizarre," explains Shell.

The results cover a hilarious and won-derfully creative length and breadth of inspirations, from world-famous buildings to historical and mythological personages to signs of the zodiac to natural disasters (the Titanic, for instance, attends the ball with her date, the Iceberg). All are accom-plished with the same stunning artistry and wit that Bob Ringwood and Mary Vogt brought to their extensive and extraordinary work for *Batman Returns*.

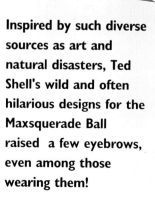

Inspired by such diverse sources as art and natural disasters, Ted Shell's wild and often hilarious designs for the Maxsquerade Ball raised a few eyebrows, even among those wearing them!

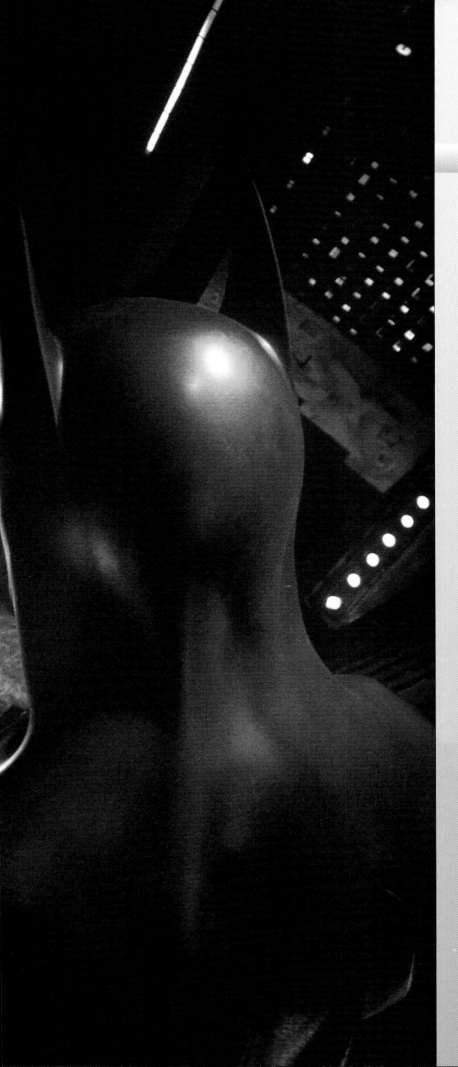

SPECIAL FX

There are special effects...and there are *special* effects! What Tim Burton and Denise Di Novi wanted for *Batman Returns* was state-of-the-art movie magic from the best of the best. Visual effects supervisor Michael Fink decided, for the sake of both economy and efficiency, to divide the duties for creating the more than 100 special effects shots between five different award-winning production houses specializing in such cinematic wonders as articulated animal robots, computer generated imagery, intricate miniatures and marvelous matte paintings. All manner of wizardry was afoot, aloft and awebbed for the Caped Crusader's second epic adventure.

THE PENGUIN'S PENGUINS

When one thinks of creatures most utilized in motion pictures, our tuxedoed and feathered friends from the northern- and southernmost regions of the globe do not immediately spring to mind. Yet, people have an absolute fascination with penguins. Just check out their pavilions at zoos and aquatic theme parks and see the goggle-eyed throngs gathered to watch their extraordinary gracefulness in the water (and endearing awkwardness on land).

For *Batman Returns*, Tim Burton required not a flock of penguins, but an army...literally! In the story, Danny DeVito's Penguin commands battalions of Penguin Commandos, programmed to execute his every order.

But where in the world does one cast an army of penguins? Now, *there's* a problem that Central Casting hasn't come up with a solution for as of yet. However, in the grand Hollywood tradition of creating what isn't there, the *Batman Returns* special effects sorcerers went to work.

And in the version that reaches the screen, what the audience will see is a splendid and seamless amalgamation of four separate elements: real, live, from their webs-to-their-beaks blackfoot penguins and king penguins; 30 incredibly complex penguin "puppets" – actually articulated robots – developed, constructed and operated by Stan Winston's

Above left: A Stan Winston Studios technician working out realistic articulated movements of the skeletal penguin "puppets." Top: Authentic penguin puppet heads from Winston and company...no animal products used at all! Above: Test footage of computer generated penguin imagery from Boss Films.

famed special effects studio; six complicated emperor penguin "suits," inhabited by performers of small stature; and fantastically realistic computer generated penguin imagery created by Boss Film Studios, with John Bruno supervising all of Boss' effects contributions·to the film.

It goes without saying that co-ordinating these diverse units was a monumental undertaking, but Michael Fink knew what had to be done. Namely, the impossible.

To Stan Winston, who received an Academy Award for *Aliens* (1986) and nominations for *Heartbeeps* (1981), *Predator* (1987), *Edward Scissorhands* (1990) and two for *Terminator 2: Judgment Day* (1991), "The biggest challenge in creating the army of penguins was doing the best we could to replicate real life, with anatomically and cosmetically correct penguins given the ability to perform and act under direction."

The penguin "puppets" from Winston's studio were all fabricated from non-organic materials, with the exception of dyed chicken feathers used for the tails. Created in three sizes (18-inch, 31-inch and 40-inch), each penguin came with its own personal "puppeteer." These highly talented individuals, many of them actors in their own rights, were capable of mechanically articulating the "puppets" through an intricate system of cables and radio controls. But they also had the ability to impart personality into the penguins through their performance skills.

Andy Schoneberg and Craig Caton-Largent, respectively the art and mechanical

department coordinators of the penguin puppets, carefully relayed Tim Burton's directions to the puppeteers. "It was as if Tim was the orchestra conductor and Andy and Craig were prompters," remarks puppeteer Joanne Bloomfield.

Also utilizing their acting techniques were the six extraordinary "little people" who occupied the 40-pound emperor penguin suits as the most majestic birds of all. All agreed that their extensive study of penguin behavior and movement before their on-set work began was a great help. "It was important to watch their behavior within a group, their neck movements, exactly how they walk," says Denise Killpack. "Then, when you're in costume, you visualize, remember and transform yourself."

Felix Silla, whose 30 years in show business included a stint as Cousin Itt on TV's original "The Addams Family," was glad that the suit was lined with artificial fur and feathers as protection from the Lair's air-conditioned big chill. "On the first day, I just told them to leave me in the costume," chuckles Silla. "It was nice and warm in there, but freezing on the soundstage."

The only problems facing both puppeteers and emperor penguin performers were when the *real* penguins took a more than passing interest in them. This might include a friendly peck on the beak, or something a little more aggressively territorial!

By and large, though, the blackfoot and king penguins truly won over the entire cast and crew. Lovingly raised and cared for by humans (the blackfoots by *Batman Returns* animal trainer Gary Gero, and the kings by Richard Hill, owner of a British park in the Cotswolds known as "Birdland"), the penguins were usually quite sociable and friendly. Their waddling walk from their air-conditioned trailers (with their own pools, in true Hollywood style) to the set – and vice versa – was comically known to all as "The

Main: The Batskiboat thunders through Gotham City's sewers. Top left: Jacques Rey's pre-production drawing of this exciting sequence. Below left: 4-Ward Productions special effects artists operate the six-foot-long miniature. Above: Penguin Commandos fire their rockets at the Batskiboat.

Penguin Shuffle." And when they finished their work, there wasn't a human soul on the set who wasn't sad to bid their aquatic colleagues a last goodbye.

COMPUTER GENERATED MARVELS

Meanwhile, the creative minds at Boss Films, whose impressive credits include *Ghostbusters* (1984), *2010* (1984) and *Die Hard* (1988), utilized the most up-to-the-microsecond computer technology to enhance the film's range by expanding the Penguin Commando Army by thousands...all on chips!

And over at Video Image Associates, equally skilled computer artists were inventing generated likenesses of bats swarming over the terrified citizens of Gotham City; and the Batmobile's security cloak effect.

"Computer generated images are no longer experimental," notes Michael Fink. "It's no longer a novelty, but a well-proven method of creating extremely realistic multidimensional figures." Fink points out that the Batmobile security cloak was accomplished in the first film through the more traditional cel animation, but advances in computer technology are able to create effects that are more lifelike, and easier to do as well.

THE BATSKIBOAT AND OTHER MIRACLES

When Batman needs to get around on *terra firma*, he rockets around in the Batmobile. But when he has to get from point place to place *beneath* Gotham City – through the endless, circuitous sewers and underground waterways – he pilots the fabulously swift

Batskiboat, introduced for the first time in *Batman Returns*.

"The Batskiboat was the synthesis of many ideas," emphasizes production designer Bo Welch. "I would have to say that Jacques Rey, one of our production illustrators, probably made the biggest contribution to its final design."

Two Batskiboats were constructed, one full-scale at 25-feet-long and 16-feet-wide, and a quarter-scale miniature which was six feet long and four feet wide. 4-Ward Productions (also Academy Award nominees for their work on 1991's *Terminator 2: Judgment Day*) built the miniature, and filmed it soaring through 100 feet of scaled-down Gotham City sewers, evading missiles fired at it by the Penguin Commandos.

The model work for *Batman Returns* was also strictly top-of-the-line. Boss Films constructed and photographed dazzling models of Gotham Plaza and the Shreck Industries Building, identical in every small detail to the full-sized set.

Stetson Visual Services, who have contributed effects to such films as *Total Recall* (1990) and *Edward Scissorhands* (1990), painstakingly assembled yet another intricate miniature: the complete, old, abandoned, bizarre Gotham Zoo. 4-Ward Productions also contributed an astonishingly authentic quarter-scale miniature re-creation of the Downtown Gotham City set for the Batmissile to zoom through.

Up north in San Francisco, the artists at Matte World were painting beautifully detailed elaborations of the "real " Gotham City, immeasurably increasing its already tremendous scale.

Ultimately, according to Michael Fink, movie special effects follow the same traditions laid down some 60 years ago. "The technique is basically the same," he maintains. "The difference is not in the technique...it's in the technology!"

HOT GADGETS & COOL WHEELS

The myriad vehicles, weapons and gadgets showcased in the film are an accurate reflection of the overall design, requiring much interdepartmental co-ordination.

The terrifically imaginative designs for the vehicles, weaponry and gadgets of *Batman Returns* required a tremendous amount of inter-departmental coordination between production designer Bo Welch, transportation captain Tommy Tancharoen, visual effects supervisor Michael Fink, mechanical effects supervisor Chuck Gaspar, with prop masters Bill and Vic Petrotta also on hand to make sure that heroes and villains alike had their arsenals fully stocked.

Consistency in the design of all vehicles and weapons for Batman was the name of the game for Bo Welch, all of them based on the smooth, sleek lines of the Dark Knight's personal aesthetic.

Although the **Batmobile** (opposite) basically retains the same "menacing and intimidating" design that the late Anton Furst created for the first film, it packs several new surprises for this second adventure, including lethal, spinning, metallic **Batdiscs** (above). Ejected from an opening on opposite sides of the Batmobile, mechanical effects supervisor Chuck Gaspar and his team developed a trapshoot-like device which could rocket out as many as 15 Batdiscs, one after another, every quarter of a second.

Also re-designed is the **Batarang** (top), equipped this time with a readout screen which allows Batman to program his target. "You might call it a 'Super-Batarang,'" says Welch. The Batarang was built in three different versions: action prop, video insert and motion control models.

The Batmobile's most special new feature is held for one of the film's pre-
mier sequences...hurtling at full speed
toward a very narrow space between two
brick tenements, seconds before impact,
Batman connects some wires inside the car.
And at that moment, the side and tail sections of the Batmobile spring off (above, in
illustrator Jacques Rey's production sketch),
the wheels contract into a rollerblade con-
figuration and the Batmobile is magically
transformed into the super-streamlined
Batmissile (above right), which handily
soars between the buildings. Two separate
Batmissiles were constructed for this
thrilling scene: one full-sized and operated
by the mechanical effects department, and
another in miniature that was constructed
and filmed by Bob and Dennis Skotak's 4-
Ward Productions special effects company.

The Penguin's mode of transportation is
a whimsical, large, yellow **Duck Vehicle**
(opposite bottom and middle), its childlike
quality an ironic and even poignant contrast
to the hideous personage at the controls. An
amusement park ride re-rigged to allow The
Penguin amphibious travel through the sewers, up steep embankments, across his
watery Lair and even onto dry land, the
Duck Vehicle is also equipped with a scis-
sors-lift feature that enables this nasty sewer
bird to rise up from the bowels of Gotham
City to observe innocent citizens from within various sewer grates.

The **Red Triangle Circus Train** (opposite top) "has a real classic, turn-of-the-century period feel," says Bo Welch. In fact,
the caged cars are authentic relics of that
period. The locomotive, however, was
designed by Welch and built by legendary
car customizer George Barris (who
designed the 1966 TV Batmobile). What
Welch calls "a dirty clown design scheme"
also informs the garish **Red Triangle
Circus Gang Motorcycles** (far right top)
and the candy cane color-striped **Penguin
Commando Rockets** that are launched
from their armored packs (far right, middle
and bottom, in Tim Flattery's production
sketch and as they appear in the film).

The weapons and gadgets utilized by the three main protagonists run the gamut from high-to-low tech. Batman's **Speargun** (top left and above) is basically the same model that John Evans designed for the first film, a handy and compact item capable of firing grappling hooks with attached wires at high speed.

Brand new, however, is the **Double Grappling Hook** (center left), a completely revised version of the first movie's Gauntlet. This is a more elaborate gadget than the Speargun, allowing Batman to fire twin hooks connected to wires and pulleys, which he can ride to safety. "We wanted this gadget to have a real edge," says Bo Welch, "so the section which Batman actually grasps is designed like sleek brass knuckles."

Catwoman, on the other claw, relies on one of history's most ancient weapons...her **Whip** (opposite bottom), which she wields with deadly precision. Carefully selected for Michelle Pfeiffer was an Australian-style kangaroo whip of four different lengths. "It's a 12-grade whip that's made up of an inner core, a wrapping, then a fine braid on the outside so that it has a multiple coil of connection," explains Anthony De Longis, Pfeiffer's whip trainer. This whip becomes a completely natural extension of Catwoman's character and personality. So are her **Talons**, which give her the ability to slice, dice, rip, tear and puncture virtually any material that exists...including wood, metal and Batman's armor!

Mention The Penguin, and to a lot of Batman fans, his name is synonymous with **Umbrellas.** They look harmless when folded and resting in an umbrella rack (top), but get them into The Penguin's webbed hands, and watch out! These ignoble tools of terror include (clockwise from right) the **Flamethrower**, unleashing a virtual conflagration; the **Dazer**, which produces a "hypnotic" effect on its victim and then fires off individual shotgun rounds; the **Machine Gun**, spraying a deadly hail of bullets in rapid succession; and the **Knife**, which releases a razor-sharp and very nasty blade from its tip. Chuck Gaspar and his mechanical effects department developed the complex inner workings of the umbrellas, allowing the ignominious man-bird to unfold his particular genius for outrageous destruction.

CREDITS

CREW LIST
DIRECTOR Tim Burton
PRODUCERS Denise Di Novi, Tim Burton
CO-PRODUCER Larry Franco
ASSOC PRODUCER/PRODUCTION MANAGER Ian Bryce
EXECUTIVE PRODUCERS Jon Peters, Peter Guber,
   Benjamin Melniker, Michael Uslan
SCREENWRITERS Daniel Waters, Wesley Strick
DIRECTOR OF PHOTOGRAPHY Stefan Czapsky
PRODUCTION DESIGNER Bo Welch
ART DIRECTORS Tom Duffield, Rick Heinrichs
SET DECORATOR Cheryl Carasik
COSTUME DESIGNERS Bob Ringwood, Mary Vogt
MUSIC Danny Elfman
FILM EDITOR Chris Lebenzon
FIRST ASSISTANT DIRECTOR David McGiffert
SOUND MIXER Peter Hliddal
KEY MAKE-UP ARTIST Ve Neill
KEY HAIR STYLIST Yolanda Toussieng
VISUAL EFFECTS SUPERVISOR Michael Fink
MECHANICAL EFFECTS SUPERVISOR Chuck Gaspar
2ND UNIT DIRECTOR Billy Weber
2ND UNIT DIRECTOR/STUNT CO-ORDINATOR Max Kleven
CASTING Marion Dougherty

CAST LIST
Batman/Bruce Wayne **MICHAEL KEATON**
The Penguin/Oswald Cobblepot **DANNY DeVITO**
Catwoman/Selina Kyle **MICHELLE PFEIFFER**
Max Shreck **CHRISTOPHER WALKEN**
Alfred **MICHAEL GOUGH**
Police Commissioner Gordon **PAT HINGLE**
Mayor of Gotham City **MICHAEL MURPHY**
Ice Princess **CRISTI CONAWAY**
Chip Shreck **ANDREW BRYNIARSKI**
Organ Grinder **VINCENT SCHIAVELLI**
Jen **JAN HOOKS**
Josh **STEVE WITTING**
Swordswallower **JOHN STRONG**
Tattooed Strongman **RICK ZUMWALT**
Poodle Lady **ANNA KATARINA**
Knifethrower Dame **ERIKA ANDERSCH**
Fat Clown **TRAVIS McKENNA**
Thin Clown **DOUG JONES**
Snakewoman **FLAME**

ABOUT THE AUTHOR

MICHAEL SINGER has been known for the last ten years as the author of *Film Directors: A Complete Guide* (Lone Eagle), an annually-published film industry reference book.
As a freelance journalist, he has contributed articles to such publications as *Film Comment*, *Films in Review* and *American Cinematographer*.

ABOUT THE PHOTOGRAPHERS

ZADE ROSENTHAL was the first unit still photographer of *Batman Returns*; **DEAN WILLIAMS** was the second unit still photographer of *Batman Returns*; **JANE O'NEAL** did selected pre-production photography; **MICHAEL GARLAND** is an architectural photographer; **VIRGIL MIRANO** is the staff photographer of Boss Film Studios; photographs are also contributed by staff members of **4-WARD PRODUCTIONS.**

CREDITS NOT FINAL

Imagesetting by Alphabet Set Limited
Colour reproduction by Rival Colour